Praise for *Deep Tradeoffs*

Life brings all kinds of problems that can't be isolated and resolved. These discussions about tradeoffs are surprising, sometimes shocking, and usually novel. This is where people live, and they don't realize they live there. – John Lachs, Centennial Professor of Philosophy Emeritus, Vanderbilt University

A tour de force whose audience should include senators, corporate executives, and others responsible for setting the tone of everything from select board hearings to Instagram speech.   – David Kelley, Attorney

Deep Tradeoffs *lends itself to some wonderful conversations, reflecting the author's ability and desire to have meaty discussions with mutual respect. This is a skill much needed in today's world.* – Cheryl Bachelder, retired CEO

Warm, conversational, and balanced. That sense of conversation among an intriguing assortment of wits and sages from past and present makes eager to join in with my own thoughts. That creates a powerful engagement between the reader and the material. It's a wonderful way to illuminate ideas. It's good fodder for conversation in social situations, and a great way to bypass all the bickering among people who disagree.   – Jeanette Blair, homemaker

Small-minded people only see their side of the argument, whereas truly wise people see both sides and have a reason for choosing theirs. Rather than arguing like children, we can become more adult-like by understanding the tradeoffs and opposing views in all of the choices we make, seeing and appreciating the other side, and choosing our path with a full understanding of what we're getting and what we're giving up. – Chris Calton, entrepreneur

Wow! What an incredible distillation and exploration. I was struck by the integration of so many different themes, thinkers, theories while also being practical and personal. The writing style feels warm, accessible, clear and enjoyable. I'm always trying to look at nuance, complexity, and conflict with a gracious, creative lens, and this book encourages that process. This is really an amazing accomplishment — exciting, relevant, and thoughtful! – Counselor

Right on the mark... what's needed in today's world. Illuminating, thoughtful, amazing.   – Sandra Plant

This is how we can get along with each other. – Wilford Fuqua, retired CEO

D1545851

Deep Tradeoffs

Restoring Balance and Respect
In A Polarized, Angry World

Mike Hassell

Dedicated to Susan, Emily, and Thomas
with my love and respect.

Copyright © 2023 by Michael D. Hassell

Published by MDH, LLC dba Deep Tradeoffs Publishing

ISBN:
978-1-960774-00-2

First printing, June 2023

Find us on the web at deeptradeoffs.com

Email us at comments@deeptradeoffs.com

Table of Contents

<u>Chapters</u>

At each chapter's end are action steps and recommended additional reading.

1. **<u>Peace or Striving</u>** – for many, peace is ultimate and iconic. But struggle is inevitable when we engage in the world. Healthy conflict drives change and growth. When should we accept & submit, or confront & fight? Respect & yield, vs. criticize & resist? Mind our own business - or protest, risk, and disrupt? Struggling is *not* peaceful. If we make peace with the status quo, we abandon our agitation for positive change...............**1**

2. **Ideals or Reality** – Should we follow our dreams – or keep both feet on the ground? Is it 'idealistic' to be earnestly optimistic, or 'realistic' to be cynical and pessimistic? Many people direct attention to the spiritual, conceptual, poetic realm of the possible; others prefer the material, tangible, scientific realm of the actual. Historians and theologians testify that **reality** is rarely if ever **ideal**; we live between the worlds of *is* and *ought*. Yet we grieve or lash out angrily when our *oughts* are not realized.................**69**

3. **Honesty or Deception** – If honesty is the best policy, why so much deception? Are we being honest about how much we deceive others, and *especially ourselves*? When is deception necessary, or even beneficial?...**117**

iv

Introduction

Increasingly we live in an intellectually polarized world, becoming more intolerant, uncivil, and narrow-minded. This diminishes our capacity to solve problems, to sustain friendships, to work collaboratively, and to make good decisions.

This book is a plea to readers to reconsider how we talk to each other. It's a framework for understanding conflict, for perceiving why we behave this way. It has much to say about what we can do about it, organized around some key value conflicts.

Some of our predicament may involve our 24-7 news cycle of constant conflict, and the hit-and-run nature of social media (and even traditional media). Another factor is working and interacting remotely, living through computer screens without the real flesh and blood of regular human contact. Robert Putnam, in his book *Bowling Alone*, offers some valuable insights into this dangerous phenomenon that threatens the quality of our families, friends, educational institutions, businesses and even our government.

Others can explain why we've become this way. That's not the purpose of Mike's book.

These pages strive to offer insights into the thought processes at work especially in this not-so-brave new world. In such a world, where lives and work are increasingly connected but further and further removed from each other, Mike offers the reader a new paradigm (and many suggestions – see esp. Chapter 4) for navigating our difficult conversations. It will not be easy, but we must reconsider how we talk to each other.

David Kelley
March, 2023

David Kelley, a Vermont attorney and avid fly fisherman, co-founded PH International and the Vermont Wildlife Coalition. While a law student at Georgetown University, David worked as a proctor for Congressional Pages, including high school senior Mike Hassell. David and Mike became life-long friends by talking about the world's problems. They've been agreeing and disagreeing now for many decades.

Preface

You and I make the angels weep. Our culture makes them wail. Many think 'I know what's right and best,' and people who agree with me must win. The other side just doesn't get it.

When is the last time you heard someone say "I'm bad, wrong and unfair, while you're right, good, and fair?" In controversies, we react by defending our beliefs and digging in our heels. This tendency, known as "motivated reasoning," is pervasive and well-known to psychologists. "*Yes, but…*" is a dead giveaway: most of our thinking and arguing justifies our current beliefs, rather than creating and developing better ones. Motivated reasoning does

NOT weigh the evidence and make a reasoned conclusion. It is NOT balanced, impartial, or respectful of others. Motivated reasoning extends a subconscious reflex that says *I will win, you must lose. My* beliefs, perceptions, and commitments are right, good, and fair, and you've got a problem. We'll see much more on motivated reasoning, in several chapters.

A related human feature is *bias*, which now is an accusation: YOU are biased, confess now and submit to retraining. Yet psychologists have documented over a hundred normal biases at work in *every* human brain. Most are normal, inevitable shortcuts that our brains must use to work quickly and efficiently.

And what about prejudice? We know the harms caused by *pre-judging* a person based only on some involuntary characteristic. Yet many pre-judgments are clearly constructive, such as a belief that love is better than hate, or persuasion is preferable to force. In fact, we prejudge things all the time – unless we have learned nothing, prefer nothing, and believe nothing.

Beliefs, perceptions, preferences, biases, and prejudices can be right or wrong, constructive or destructive – but *motivated reasoning* instinctively defends our particular judgments against all comers. We "lean" or are "oriented" toward some values, yet almost every value has a conflicting alternative. Many **value conflicts** cannot be solved like a problem in math or science. Each value is inescapable, and a conflict with another value is inevitable and everlasting.

Consider the value conflicts at the heart of two hot controversies in our day, abortion and required vaccination. "*My body, my choice*" is proclaimed in both controversies, each with life and death at stake. This short phrase powerfully declares independence, demanding that I (not you, not we, not the government) must be in charge of a vital decision. Respect for **autonomy and conscience** (i.e., self-determination) are critically important values in free societies. Yet so are the **duty to avoid harm,** respect for the **rule of law,** and **respect for life**, all especially relevant for the weak or vulnerable.

Abortion _and_ vaccination involve all these conflicting values. Yet partisans left and right prioritize one value for abortion and stridently reject that value for mandated vaccination. It's common to be pro-choice and anti-resistance, OR pro-life and anti-mandate. In both cases, are we better left alone – or coerced?

Speaking of declaring independence, both abortion and vaccination powerfully impact others – sex partners and fetuses, or roommates and people in line. A rights-based claim denies that others have any standing or say in the matter. It's an insistent form of self-reliance, and a denial of majority rule. So are we islands or villages? Where does _in_dependence end, and _inter_dependence begin?

Attitudes about these conflicted choices are far too easily predicted by political affiliation. Mary from the left wants few or no restrictions on private abortion decisions, but demands vaccination mandates for all. John from the right is all about restricting abortions, yet nobody shall command what vaccines he must take. If by a wild miracle John and Mary agree on autonomy for abortion AND vaccinations, then we might ask: should their child's school be freely chosen or mandated? Who can choose or authorize surgery to change gender? Can the terminally ill (or their caregivers) choose euthanasia? What are my choices in selling or buying body parts, blood, drugs, or sex? May I carry a gun and shoot someone who threatens grave harm to me, my family, or another person? In short: which choices are personal, and which are to be controlled by others?

There are reasons to affirm or oppose autonomy in each of these matters. Most people favor autonomy for this but control for that. We reflexively choose sides, then renounce or rebuke any choice that conflicts with our own.

Did _you_ respond reflexively in simply reading these controversial questions? We need better instincts than "I'm right and good, you're wrong and bad."

Applying principles... inconsistently

Most of us *strive* to be fair and even-handed. We want to follow reasonable laws that constrain everyone fairly. Isn't it true that "what's good for the goose is good for the gander," so rules for John must also apply to Mary? Yet we know it's very common for people to apply principles *inconsistently.* What may be surprising is that inconsistency is not always hypocritical or wrong.

Most sweeping rules have reasonable exceptions. Many subtleties and nuances shape how we apply principles – or refuse to apply them – in a world too complex for simple, universal rules. For example, New Yorkers need very different rules and regulations than ranchers in rural Wyoming. Greater legal differences are necessary in the Australian outback or Himalayan mountains, on the sea or in space. The idea of a national minimum wage, much less a global or interplanetary one, is simply absurd. One size does not fit all. Simply put: few rules can be universal. We are too different, and our circumstances are way too different, for the same specific rules to be applied everywhere.

Yet legal equality – the equal *application* of law – is a bedrock of justice. How could we possibly reconcile this contradiction? What can it mean to equally apply the same rules for everyone in a big, diverse country or world? How can we act in a principled way amid so many variations and exceptions?

Almost all of us work to preserve our belief that we've gotten all of this right, and John or Mary not so much. We may fight to justify Mary's green light and John's red light, or vice versa. We fight to inconsistently apply the rules, predictably favoring the outcomes we want (or that our political party wants).

Let's acknowledge a basic truth: people are often *partial,* and sometimes even *unfair.* We shouldn't expect otherwise. We know each of us has beliefs, prejudices, and biases; being confident about our priorities tells us how to behave. Yet in acting on our cherished opinions and principles, it's a challenge to respect conflicting opinions, principles, and choices. Those who haven't reached fighting mode often evade conflict with dodgy lip service, "agreeing to disagree," or just silence. Evading a bitter fight is a worthy outcome, but resentments and frustrations can live on like poisonous snakes in the grass, waiting to strike. Some of these threats can be de-fanged by mutuality, willingness to listen, and maybe even forgiveness.

Many of us want (but can't find) some way to turn down the heat, to reduce alienation and bickering. We struggle to find peace of mind. But we also want to do something constructive about rampant disagreements. We want peace and harmony, but improving things will require non-peaceful struggle. It will require careful, skillful striving and testy conflict management rather than running away from our differences or fighting to the death:

> *Many of us look at conflict as something we'd rather avoid than engage in with confidence. But conflict and disagreement can be quite beneficial.*
> – Francesca Gino, Harvard Business School

The good news is that there's an obvious, but not easy, way to discover overlooked pieces of truth. We can prepare ourselves to look more closely at what's offered by people who disagree with us – those who defend a deep value that conflicts with a deep value we favor. We can look for something to accept among the things that an opponent treasures. There are so many overlooked insights and respectable views to be discovered out there, on both sides of most any issue. Many overlooked tidbits are presented in this book through quotes from insightful people. Some embrace your dearest values and others express a directly conflicting alternative.

Better understanding a valid alternative reveals new possibilities for reconciling deep conflicts, at least in part. Clearly seeing and respecting other deeply held convictions can subdue the sharp elbows we're throwing.

Submerged Dualities are Deep Tradeoffs

Deep tradeoffs between key values lurk persistently in the background, behind our daily dozens of more mundane tradeoffs (pro/con, cost/benefit, price/quality, now/later, risk/reward, work/life, rent/make/buy, and so on). Deeper beliefs and values are entrenched, committed, sustained, and sturdy. We fight for them, usually unaware of how much other important values can compete with (or contradict) our core values. It's as if life's instruction book somewhere says that virtue requires us to 'line up alphabetically by height.' Each way of ordering has its merits and problems, but we merrily (or angrily) insist on one or the other. Over time, as circumstances change, some switch their priorities among deep tradeoffs, much like swing voters:

- Today we demand new laws to control, tomorrow we deregulate and liberate.

- Sometimes we reason and impartially analyze; other times we're passionate fanatics, out to win.

- Idealist Bob is committed to achieving a more perfect world. But sometimes he sees the merit in Jane's realism (that shortcomings are inevitable, we're *not* perfectible, and it's harmful to pretend every problem is solvable with better laws, budgets, or elected officials).

- Sue wants more equality or equity. But sometimes she respects Mark's demand for liberty and difference. In many ways Sue also wants simply to be left alone to live her unique dream.

- We're individuals in diverse groups. Some identify as one among many, others as cogs in a big machine. This simple choice has huge consequences.

These deeper, value-laden tradeoffs provide powerful lenses for evaluating what's unseen, or vaguely understood, behind our daily struggles. Often our "truths" are half-truths, meaning they're true in *some sense* but not in others, or in *some situations* and not others. Neither side of a tradeoff captures the whole truth. Half-truths may very well outnumber truths and lies combined, as we'll discuss in our chapter on Honesty and Deception.

Searching for competing values also gives us a permanently useful way to find more balance and insight. Many problems could be eased with more symmetric, even-minded thinking. This is not to say we should be constantly wishy washy, equivocal, or spineless. It is to say we should relax our blinders, letting in some light that might illuminate opportunities for minor *agreement*. A small agreement, even a petty one, is a first step toward reconciliation, or even friendship.

Good people lean strongly toward one option in these tradeoffs, but many also can see the reasonableness of a conflicting choice. One-eyed advocates (possibly fanatics, including ourselves) make a habit of one perspective. Yet in quieter moments, away from the confrontations, each of our passionate selves can more fully acknowledge a competing priority, another way of choosing.

People are simply **poor critics of their own thoughts and behavior.** This is important enough to repeat in the words of an ancient proverb: we **see a speck in another person's eye, but don't notice the log in our own eye**. Instead of repeatedly looking for reasons to support and defend what we already believe or do, let's try a different way.

***

Conflict is Inevitable, But People can Reconcile

Some people appear outraged by hard disagreements. Dramatic news reports suggest we should be shocked – shocked!!! – by conflict and argument. **Our stress levels might be lowered simply by expecting conflicts to be normal and inevitable... par for the course**. Better understanding *other paths* can deeply expose what we're getting, and what we're giving up, in the choices we've made and in the values we favor.

We crave a *right answer*. We fight those whose right answer crosses ours. Wouldn't it be much better to acknowledge trade-offs – to respect the person who weighs alternatives differently – then discuss how to balance *more than one* right answer? Plural values are not new or unfamiliar; we know them well indeed. Our challenge is to defang the tensions between the things most of us hold dear, but with differing priorities and degrees of intensity or skepticism.

Maybe our ultimate goal can become not necessarily victory, but some reconciliation with others. This was the case in one of the greatest, most polarizing cultural struggles of the 20th century:

> *The ultimate goal of every civil-rights campaign, from the Montgomery bus boycott in 1955 to the Freedom Rides in 1961 to the march in Selma, was not victory but reconciliation. That made it important not to alienate fence-sitters, Black or white. For instance, Birmingham's small Black middle class did not support the civil-rights campaign there, but its members were still briefed on operations, so they would understand what was happening and why... the movement was essentially teaching white southerners how to live in a post-segregation world.*
>
> – Thomas E. Ricks, author, *Waging a Good War: A Military History of the Civil Rights Movement, 1954-1968.*

With respectful friendships, we are much more likely to cooperatively find solutions, and maybe even common ground. **When we accept that our most stubborn and annoying conflicts are healthy and inevitable, rather than an existential battle – our toxic behaviors and attitudes can morph into something far more constructive.**

Accepting rivalry and competitive values is an alternative to being stuck with only one set of right answers:

Acceptance is the door into reality… when you fall out of 'accept,' you're back to stuck. – D. Evans & B. Burnett, *Designing Your Life*

As we'll try to show in this book, the reality about deep tradeoffs is that:

- people have different conclusions about many conflicting values
- most people, notably our opponents, are not stupid or evil
- value conflicts aren't going away
- neither side should impose value preferences in a free society
- it's better to manage or settle differences than to vanquish opponents

The Benefits of Symmetry

Tradeoffs require us to **think *symmetrically***. Amid so much disagreement and strife, mirrored thinking exposes new possibilities for balance, broader perspectives, even friendship. Symmetrical thinking helps us to:

1. Make **better choices** by grasping alternative (even contradictory) values, and the merits of each
2. **Relate better** to friends, acquaintances, or opponents who have different values and beliefs
3. **Communicate better**, beginning conversations with a better sense of where others may be coming from
4. **Understand almost any value has a legitimate alternative** that a reasonable person might choose
5. Decode rants by **seeing the invisible alternative** that's typically hidden from listeners who lack balanced insights
6. Be more effective in **debate, argument, problem solving, and decision making**
7. **Take conflict more readily in stride** – and be at peace with it

Deep Tradeoffs offers two other key benefits. By **entering the conversation of great thinkers** (quoted extensively here), you can use their examples in better discussions with your friends. Along the way you'll gain a more **practical view of transcendent topics** like Happiness, Community, Imagination, Freedom, Peace, Truth, and more – all seen through the lens of perennial tradeoffs.

Long Traditions of Balancing Binaries

Deep tradeoffs reflect eternal conflicts within the human condition. These conflicts can't be prevented or resolved, but they can be managed. Lawyer and author Dean Spader calls this the *"golden zigzag between conflicting fundamental values."* Political theorist Isaiah Berlin said that when two good ideas compete *"we are doomed to choose, and every choice may entail an irreparable loss."* Abraham Lincoln had this problem in spades; he believed that a tightrope walker best symbolized his predicament in an America torn in two.

As we proceed in a discussion between writer and reader – hopefully revealing some building blocks for great conversations with friends – remember that Americans follow in a great tradition of balancing binaries:

> *America has generally expanded its idea of itself, and broadened its democracy, by struggling through conflicts of its contending faiths, value systems and ethnic components: thesis, antithesis, synthesis. It is as if the country came with an embedded scheme of binaries—colonial revolutionaries vs. loyalists, immigrants vs. nativists, whites vs. blacks, old Eastern elites vs. Western Jacksonians, North vs. South, rural vs. urban, wets vs. dries, labor vs. management, and so on—that had to be fought over and resolved.* — Walter Russell Mead

A journalist and former magazine essayist puts it in the present tense:

> *Everywhere you look in the American drama, you see doubles banging against each other.* — Lance Morrow

An Irish poet sees doubles *within* each of us:

> *The work of peace is to recognize that even in every individual, there are so many plurals.*
> — Pádraig Ó Tuama

Once alerted to deep tradeoffs, we see them everywhere, past and present. We confront differences and choices repeatedly. It's a particularly American way of life: our founders brilliantly structured the way we manage trade-offs, with checks and balances on power in three co-equal branches of government. The founders' primary goal was to make it supremely hard for any side to dominate – tyranny. They especially feared the tyranny of the majority.

Poet Robert Frost, in *The Road Not Taken*, beautifully expressed the impact of essential choices:

> *Two roads diverged in a yellow wood,*
> *And sorry I could not travel both…*
> *I took the one less traveled by,*
> *And that has made all the difference.* – Robert Frost

Here Frost remembers a life path chosen long before, with vast consequences. But value tradeoffs are *ongoing* rival paths that we **continually choose and rechoose.** Many of us wear one path deep and wide – sometimes called a rut. Better understanding *other paths* helps us see what we're getting and what we're giving up. Other choices have beauty to offer; they are valid alternatives to the path we're on. We need to be more aware of them.

Respecting Contradictions Through Even-Handed Perspectives

To better understand anything, we can probe what opposes or contradicts it. Knowing more about value tradeoffs makes them jump from daily news and conversations. As one side is presented, we also begin to perceive the hidden, balancing alternative. Even-handed perspectives can deliver peace of mind to sparring advocates, who otherwise simply continue to torment each other:

So much of what we call human depravity ("evil") seems to be based on a principle termed "the polarized mind." The polarized mind is the fixation on a single point of view to the utter exclusion of competing points of view, and it has caused more human torment and misery than virtually any other factor.

– Kirk Schneider & Sayyad Fatemi, Scientific American magazine

Consider this book as an invitation to debate and reflect – NOT essays on what to think, or who to fight. There's plenty of room to disagree here, as we isolate and examine the trade-offs that underlie our never-ending struggles. Chapter 4 summarizes potential actions to deal with those struggles.

Respectful disagreement can be a healthy comparison of perspectives and experiences, NOT the moral failure that some people see in normal conflict. We don't have to think what others think, but it helps to see what others see. Also it's far easier (and vastly more pleasant) to examine differences in a spirit of cooperative friendship rather than embattled hostility.

Also consider reading *Deep Tradeoffs* in sections. If you're intrigued or provoked, put down the pages to sketch your own thoughts and questions, then discuss it all with friends. This book is presented in an intentionally compressed style, with limited length, robust indexes, and an expansive table of contents, all intended to provide quick, easy access to topics and tools that can support better conversations.

Meaningful, respectful, openly curious dialogue is a terrific way to improve and deepen relationships, especially among people who disagree. This can be as rewarding as it is rare. *Respectful* disagreement is profoundly constructive and deeply satisfying – an achievement. It just requires some effort and emotional exposure.

Great thinkers, many quoted here, have had much to say about the values, choices, and conflicts we'll discuss. We'll use them to **refine our sensitivities and habits to see symmetries anew. We'll uncover ways to repeatedly find balances within ourselves and among others**.

Some whimsical words from a New Orleans musician hint at the even-keeled mindset we'll be developing:

> *Ya never too hot, never too cold, never too young, never too old*
> *never too skinny, never too fat, never too dis, never too dat*
> *ya just where ya are,& dat's where it's at.*
>
> – Dr. John

MDH
May 5, 2023

Chapter 1 – Peace or Striving

A quiet and modest life brings more joy than a pursuit of success bound with constant unrest… a simple and unassuming life is good for everybody, physically and mentally.

– Albert Einstein

The credit belongs to the man who is actually in the arena, whose face is marred by dust and sweat and blood; who strives valiantly; who errs, and comes short again and again, because there is no effort without error and shortcoming; … who spends himself in a worthy cause; who at the best knows in the end the triumph of high achievement, and who at the worse, if he fails, at least fails while daring greatly, so that his place shall never be with those cold and timid souls who know neither victory or defeat.

– Teddy Roosevelt, at the Sorbonne, April 23, 1910

As the 21st century began, I met with colleagues one excited morning in a sunny office. Jack, an accomplished biotech researcher, had led a university department in creating a new drug for sepsis, a blood infection. A septic crisis drives the immune system into a frenzy, a "cytokine storm." Unless the storm is arrested, victims die suddenly from their own immune response. It's either a 'death by friendly fire,' or then a fight with the infection itself.

I'd been chosen to help launch a new company to commercialize this exciting new therapy. It was the kind of opportunity I lived for: to work with very smart people on a potential solution to a big problem. We'd be helping to snatch life from the jaws of death. While waiting for a lawyer's instructions to sign papers, a colleague turned to me and declared:

1

In this life, we choose between boredom and torment. Mike, you and I have chosen torment. — Earl R.

Though stunned in the moment, time and reflection have led me to appreciate Earl's insight. Torment is a price we pay for striving. Earl knew we were signing up for a long, conflict-ridden struggle. My lighter outlook had been blinded by can-do optimism. Earl set me straight.

How many of us clearly know what we want *and* how much we're willing to sacrifice or compromise to get it? We face these two simple questions thousands of times. Few things are more essential than adjusting our choices to balance effort or ease, pain or pleasure, fighting or accepting, doing or being. Repeatedly we choose to strive or to seek peace.

Almost everyone wants peace at least in some form. We know that achieving or opposing can be grueling, even painful. Yet a keen observer of our culture has noticed that people admire striving more than comfortable satisfaction:

When you read a biography of someone you admire, it's rarely the things that made them happy that compel your admiration. It's the things they did to court unhappiness — the things they did that were arduous and miserable, which sometimes cost them friends and aroused hatred. It's excellence, not happiness, that we admire most.
— David Brooks

A respected industrial scientist expressed this view exquisitely when his daughter asked "are you happy?":

Why would I want to be happy? I want to be successful.
— Dr. Ying Kao Lee

Lee's daughter, Prof. Angela Duckworth, has become a groundbreaking researcher on a characteristic of successful people that's more important than talent – what she calls Grit. (More about that later!)

Albert Einstein, despite preferring the quiet life, agreed that peaceful happiness should not be our goal or endpoint. His guiding light was found in pursuing noble ideals:

> *I have never looked upon ease and happiness as ends in themselves –*
> *this ethical basis I call the ideal of a pigsty. The ideals which have*
> *lighted my way, and time after time have given me courage to face*
> *life cheerfully, have been Kindness, Beauty, and Truth.*
>
> – Albert Einstein

Think of the millions of parents (including myself) who've said "I just want my child to be happy." What then should we tell those children about the struggle to become successful? Mothers remind their children repeatedly for years to complete homework assignments, redo botched chores, and practice, practice, practice. Those conversations typically are not peaceful or happy; noses and grindstones come to mind. Yet I'm grateful for struggles that my mother inflicted on me. The values instilled have remained long after their price was forgotten.

Some historical periods have been described as golden ages of peace and stability. Other times are revolutionary. We continually confront this question: Is happiness found in tranquility, or in pursuing change? Should we submit and rest (like a dove), or restlessly persist and resist (like a hawk)? Launch or quit? Swim or float? Compete or sell out? Fortunately, sages and poets across several millennia have shed bits of wisdom on this quandary about outer and inner action. We also have newer insights from psychological research in the 20th and 21st centuries.

Sages and Wisdom Traditions

For thousands of years, spiritual leaders have counseled a commitment to peace. Christians celebrate and pursue "*the peace of Christ.*" Muslims greet each other in Arabic, *Salaam alaikum* ("peace be upon you"). The Hebrew word for peace, *shalom* (related to Arabic *salaam*) means much more than the opposite of war. *Shalom* is wholeness or completeness, including well-being, goodwill, prosperity, and social harmony. Observant Jews seek it daily. Some idealize it as a kind of perfection, a dream to be achieved when the Messiah returns and delivers marvels of peace, at least metaphorically:

> *They shall beat their swords into plowshares, and their spears into pruning hooks; nation shall not lift up sword against nation, neither shall they learn war anymore. (Isaiah 2:4)... The wolf shall lie down with the lamb... and the nursing child shall play over the hole of the asp.* — (Isaiah 11:6-8)

The Buddha also advocated radical peace. He taught that earthly turmoil comes from desire, and called his followers to find release from all appetites. He said detaching from desire will achieve salvation, enlightenment... nirvana. The Buddha's fourth and highest trance went well beyond a peaceful mind to completely erase pain and pleasure:

> *[It was a state] which is without pain or pleasure, and with purity of mindfulness and equanimity.* — Siddhartha Gautama, the Buddha

Ancient poetry describes how becoming the Buddha completely extinguished Gautama's yearning:

> *My mind, its elements dissolved, the end of cravings has attained.* — Dhamapada (The Sayings of the Buddha)

4

Similar extremes are found in Christian monastics who make vows of poverty. Like entranced Buddhists, they often depend on others to provide life's material necessities. Resignation from the world is found among Hindus as well; the *Bhagavad Gita* has been described as a veritable treatise on non-attachment.

Yet our common experience shows that people readily abandon peace to fight for a righteous cause. Judaism, Christianity and Islam (the three religions of Abraham) call for justice and struggle to defeat evil. The word *righteous* appears in some form more than 500 times in the Bible! Jesus himself, sometimes called the "Prince of Peace," was said to demand that a follower renounce family and join the fight:

> *Do not think that I have come to bring peace to the earth. I have not come to bring peace, but a sword.* [35] *For I have come to set a man against his father, and a daughter against her mother, and a daughter-in-law against her mother-in-law.* [36] *And a person's enemies will be those of his own household.* – Matthew 10:34-36

Righteous struggle in its highest form can be peaceful, but of course it's often restless or violent. Biblical history is full of righteous wars, a pattern that lasted well into the Middle Ages with the Christian Crusades. Righteous Christian violence persisted into recent centuries in the confident religious fervor of colonialism. Mohammed too, after failing to attract voluntary converts to his movement in the early 600s A.D., resorted to about a dozen violent conquests before he died in 632. To this day, Muslim attacks often feature the cry *Allahu Akbar* (God is Greater!) – a tragic use of religious words that Muslims use elsewhere to *peacefully* affirm life and its blessings.

Peace researcher Johan Galtung notes that every religion has dual values – and conflicting commitments – to peace and to righteous struggle:

Every religion contains, in varying degrees, elements of the soft and the hard. For the sake of world peace, dialogue within religions and among them must strengthen the softer aspects. – Johan Galtung

In nearly all times and places, violence and killing have been rationalized – said to be necessary and justified – when an ultimate value is thought to be at stake. An obvious example of a cause worth fighting for is <u>survival</u> (sometimes conceived spiritually as salvation). Another example is <u>deliverance from slavery</u> or other forms of subjection. Poets, folklorists, religious leaders, and philosophers have all waded into these waters.

The famed Stoics were like-minded Greek and Roman thinkers, including even some Emperors. Stoics were well-known supporters of standing down from confrontation, accepting things as they come:

Do not seek to have things happen as you want them to, but instead want them to happen as they do happen, and your life will go well.
– Epictetus

Over time, "stoic" has come to refer to a person or an attitude that's radically accepting, indifferent to pain or pleasure, unattached to either grief or joy. Somewhat like non-attachment for Buddhists and Hindus, Stoics repress feelings and patiently endure setbacks – embracing duty, morality, and purpose rather than seeking pleasure and enjoyment.

In 17th century London, the Puritan John Bunyan cautioned that all striving for material comfort is a bad substitute for a peaceful, settled mind:

If we have not quiet in our minds, outward comfort will do no more for us than a golden slipper on a gouty foot. – John Bunyan

Aesop, the ancient teller of fables, also preferred a restful, simple life:

A crust eaten in peace is better than a banquet partaken in anxiety.
                                                        – Aesop

Peace of mind was a priority for a middle-class Texan in 2020 as he reflected on the downward spiral of a troubled Hollywood star. That celebrity's legal wrangling, failed marriage, and other struggles threatened to consume his career and enormous fortune, his reputation, and his future:

All that mess with his ex-wife makes me glad to have a grilled cheese sandwich while sitting on the couch and watching TV with my dog.
                                                        – Greg Hassell

Yet calm comfort is readily disturbed by our desire for pleasure, and wrecked by our ambition for control. A 16th-century English poet, John Dryden, expressed the determination to continue fighting after a defeat:

> *I am a little hurt but I am not slain*
> *I will lay me down to bleed for a while*
> *Then I'll rise and fight with you again.* – John Dryden

In the 18th century, American patriots blasted away at their English cousins, clearly in no mood to make peace:

If you love wealth more than liberty, the tranquility of servitude better than the animating contest of freedom, depart from us in peace. We ask not your counsel nor your arms. Crouch down and lick the hand that feeds you. May your chains rest lightly upon you and may posterity forget that you were our countrymen.

– Samuel Adams

Those who would give up essential liberty, to purchase a little temporary safety, deserve neither liberty nor safety.

– Benjamin Franklin

What country can preserve its liberties, if its rulers are not warned from time to time, that this people preserve the spirit of resistance? Let them take arms... What signify a few lives lost in a century or two? The tree of liberty must be refreshed from time to time with the blood of patriots and tyrants. It is its natural manure.

– Thomas Jefferson

Yet Jefferson also praised the peaceful life filled with useful activity. In this different mood, he indicated that happiness is produced not by striving and fighting but rather by freedom from disturbances:

It is neither wealth nor splendor; but tranquility and occupation which give happiness.   – Thomas Jefferson

Tranquility can co-exist with a spirit of resistance, perhaps as different moods on various occasions. But fighting involves actions that are clearly unaligned with most concepts of "being happy."

In the following 19th century, the English thinker and civil servant John Stuart Mill echoed Franklin and Adams – and one of Jefferson's moods – in denouncing people who prefer safety and comfort over exertion, risk, and suffering:

8

War is an ugly thing, but not the ugliest of things; the decayed and degraded state of moral and patriotic feeling which thinks nothing worth a war, is worse. A man who has nothing which he cares more about than he does about his personal safety is a miserable creature who has no chance at being free, unless made and kept so by the exertions of better men than himself. – John Stuart Mill

Many people categorically reject war. Some believe in peace at all costs, that war is senseless, and violence has never solved anything. Yet war has overthrown the tyrannies of slavery, communism, fascism, and colonialism; it has toppled genocidal dictators and autocrats. War saved highly developed countries like France and England from subjugation. Of course, some tyrants are deposed *without* full-scale war. A key question is whether violence is required – and if it is, in what circumstances and how much.

England's Winston Churchill, facing this question in 1941, magnificently stiffened the resolve of a civilization whose very existence was threatened:

Never give in, never give in, never, never, never, never - in nothing, great or small, large or petty - never give in except to convictions of honor and good sense. Never yield to force; never yield to the apparently overwhelming might of the enemy. – Winston Churchill

Fighting is most clearly justified when lives are threatened by predatory aggressors, within nature or civilization:

Everyone has an inner warrior ready to emerge, particularly when survival is at stake. The gentlest mother's inner warrior will erupt if her child is threatened. – Karl Merlantes

Cries for peace and harmony are simply misplaced when survival or subjection are at stake. Yet in each case we might ask: what really constitutes subjection or freedom? What really threatens our "survival," literally or figuratively? Sometimes we fight fiercely (if not violently) to defend our political ideas when our "survival" is simply not in question. Do political disappointments or social irritations really call for the snarling they provoke? And can snarling actually solve the problem?

Consider the development of cancel culture. People who have been cancelled certainly feel the domination being directed their way. But how much intimidation should they tolerate? What degree of condemnation, oppression, or control is equivalent to an assault? Are there acceptable tactics for controlling disliked speech? One journalist, Jason Gay, says we have a "national tantrum culture." Another points out that the stakes in our righteous disputes are about much more than civility and disallowed words:

> *In the natural world, we don't all agree; [cancel culture is a] subversion or a perversion of the natural order of things. At its heart cancel culture is about the most powerful of all battles: the conquest of the human spirit... You start to get the sense that you are outnumbered and that everyone agrees with these people, and it's completely and utterly false... The only victory that has to be given, that cannot be taken from anyone, is surrender. And the conquering of the human spirit is the ultimate battle in any fight.*
>
> – Lara Logan, broadcast journalist

Logan's contempt for cancel culture rivals the canceller's hatred for "false" words. But there's a useful distinction here: cancel culture is clearly coercive, while speech within decent limits coerces no one. You could walk away from disagreeable speech, but not from laws, rules, and domineering attacks.

If we <u>overstate</u> a "threat" or too broadly define "subjection," we invite more fighting and hostility. English political philosopher Thomas Hobbes spoke of a "state of nature" where lives are *nasty, brutish and short.*" Today's equivalent is hellish bickering and domination, escaped only at death.

But if we <u>understate</u> the injustices of an unfair world – *when* (not if) we get this wrong – we'll have at best a fragile truce. Resistance will rise again.

Most of us try to balance what to accept and what to confront. Some spew hostile judgments about things they didn't witness, and announce hatred for people they don't know. They may defend their discordant words as free speech. But they may not like the freely spoken words of those targets who feel unable to resign from a bitter confrontation they didn't choose.

***

So who decides what's more harmful – disagreeable words, or shutting off those words? The U.S. Constitution's First Amendment says only what the U.S. Congress shall not do: "*Congress shall make no law… abridging the freedom of speech, or of the press.*" The First Amendment does not say what others shall (or shall not) do. That's addressed by later court decisions that extend free speech principles particularly to state governments.

Far beyond the authority of law, culture is something we all need to respectfully critique and adjust, wherever we might have some influence. Debate over advisable speech is not new: the young George Washington had a list of rules for civil behavior, such as "*mock not nor jest at anything of importance.*" Washington's rule is now routinely violated by thousands daily, often for sport. Even children's verse has addressed uncivil speech: *sticks and stone may break my bones, but words will never hurt me.* Today the 'stiff upper lip' ethic is overturned by attention to how words can hurt. We're told that "violence" extends far beyond physical aggression to include harsh words. Some even claim that silence is violence.

A starting point for living with such conundrums is to acknowledge that perfect peace and fairness, like many other ideals, are beyond our reach:

We live in a perpetual tsunami of organized conflict.

– Jon Meacham

When human beings live together, conflict is inevitable – war is not.

– Daisaku Ikeda

There is, in fact, no such thing as peace - merely arrested conflict.

– Andrew Sullivan

Most disputes don't involve survival or tyranny, even if we characterize them that way (perhaps with cliché-ridden name-calling about a "Nazi" or "Hitler"). Yet that just makes it a closer call when we choose among less vivid choices. In a lower-stakes dispute, without Hitler around, it takes keen discernment to decide whether to challenge or submit. When do we hold onto our dreams – or settle? Should I insist on my way – or compromise?

Our default mechanisms for addressing daily, close-run disputes should not be a reflexive resort to new laws, cold wars (or hot ones), media squabbles, and social media snark. We need to pick our battles and carefully choose the ways we fight them. Often we should not fight at all, especially when we're simply angry and the chances to improve or benefit are vanishingly small:

The art of being wise is the art of knowing what to overlook.

– William James

One religious leader used a clever formula to stay out of the constant fray:

See everything, overlook a great deal, correct a little.

– Pope John XXIII

12

Greek mythology describes an opposite approach, when Zeus's wife Hera sent two snakes into the crib of the infant Hercules. The snakes were meant to kill an infant son that Zeus had fathered by a mistress. Speaking generally, confronting problems when they're small can be good strategy. But taken too far, that's a formula for becoming a know-it-all busybody.

De-escalating (as Pope John did) usually is good counsel. Yet consciously overlooking an emerging problem clearly risks allowing the problem to grow into a serious threat (such as sexual abuse in religious or corporate settings). Notice that Pope John's little motto exuded confidence in knowing what's correct for himself *and* for others. During his earlier days, when he was Angelo Giuseppe Roncalli – 4th child of 13 in a sharecropping family – Angelo might have more readily admitted that he lacked some answers. Even for Popes – indeed, for all of us – humility and modesty are good companions for de-escalating our never-ending disagreements.

Insights from Psychology and Medicine

Happiness has long been associated in the popular mind with pleasure, leisure, and escaping burdens or duties. Vacations are times of contented disengagement, enjoying a deserved reward after steady toil. Holidays are a slow, *passive* respite from busy, nose-grinding effort. The age-old priority for taking a periodic breather is embedded in *sabbath,* a regularly scheduled day of rest and escape. The enforced rest of sabbath was once legally established in "blue laws," which required businesses to close on the sabbath (long before the concept of 24/7 was invented). Our human need for a routine get-away is well expressed not only in ancient scripture, but also in today's American jargon:

13

I spend so much of my week doing things that make me feel stressed out and generally kind of unhappy. I just need a day where I'm like, you know what, screw it. I don't care if the dishes get done.

— Alex Dahl

We need rest and respite more than ever in our "always on" culture of constant availability. However, research shows that a *passive* understanding of happiness is at best misleading and incomplete. At worst, it's just plain wrong. Passive behavior, like napping or watching television, simply is NOT where most of us should expect to find lasting fulfillment. Rather, we find meaning and purpose in actively engaging and solving problems, bypassing obstacles, seizing opportunities – all those things that lie between us and a better life. One study showed this by assessing not only what people say, but also how they move:

Individuals who are more physically active are happier, [and] are happier in the moments when they are more physically active. These results emerged when assessing activity subjectively, via self-report, or objectively, via participants' smartphone accelerometers. Overall, this research suggests that not only exercise but also non-exercise physical activity is related to happiness.

— *Happier People Lead More Active* Lives
(Lathia, Sandstrom, Mascolo, & Rentfrow)

In 1990, psychologist Mihaly Csikszentmihalyi published *Flow: The Psychology of Optimal Experience*. This compelling work summarized his two decades of study on how people reach a contented state of mind: feelings of enjoyment, satisfaction, and happiness, a state called *Flow*. Athletes describe this feeling as "being in the zone," and it has nothing to do with leisure. Rather, *Flow* has everything to do with mental engagement and absorbed attention, even to the point of losing track of time.

14

Csikszentmihalyi's research showed that flow experiences occur mostly when people are actively engaged, not passively at rest. His findings were consistent with an ancient Greek definition of happiness as "*the full use of your powers along lines of excellence*" (which is John F. Kennedy's excellent paraphrase of Aristotle's fussier, opaque-in-translation remarks about excellence). Aristotle's definition declares that human flourishing is not found in passivity or leisure, but rather in the act of striving for things that are meaningful or satisfying. Of course, success is sweet – but even in failure we can be happy if we've done our best, giving our all in a worthwhile, fair struggle. "Left it all on the field," as the sportscasters say.

The bias to action extends even to the simple *physical* activities that now are known to be a key factor in sustaining mental agility, especially among the aged. Physical exercise is even better than mental puzzles for staying mentally sharp. A physician and a professor have concisely observed that at any age, we must *use or lose* our capacity for physical activity:

Life is movement. – Dr. Ed Settle

Inactivity is the enemy. – John Kaag, Professor of philosophy

Action, Achievement and Meaning

The psychologist Jonathan Haidt probed the psychology of well-being in his 2006 book, *The Happiness Hypothesis*. Haidt discusses Stoic, Buddhist, and other formulas for happiness, and relates them to the latest insights from research on what leads to happiness. One of Haidt's key conclusions is well summarized in his quote from an English novelist, who squarely rejects the restful peace that Jefferson and Einstein recommend:

It is vain to say that human beings ought to be satisfied with tranquility: they must have action; and they will make it if they cannot find it. — Charlotte Bronte, 1847

15

Haidt notes that "vital engagement" is a relationship between people and their surroundings. This vitality is driven by our innate drive to influence our circumstances, and maybe even to control them:

> *There's overwhelming evidence that people and many other mammals have a basic drive to make things happen... You can see it in the joy infants take with "busy boxes"... and in the lethargy that often overtakes people who stop working. Psychologist Robert White called it the "effectance motive..." Effectance is almost as basic a need as food and water [and] is a constant presence in our lives.*
>
> – Jonathan Haidt

Passionate engagement plays a critical role in a fulfilled life:

> *[Csikszentmihalyi showed that] paragons of success [are] people who seem to have crafted lives for themselves built around a consuming passion. These are admirable lives, desirable lives, the sort that many young people dream of having.* – Jonathan Haidt

A great Danish thinker agrees:

> *The ideal of a persistent striving is the only view of life that does not carry with it an inevitable disillusionment.* – Søren Kierkegaard

Now we can see Einstein more clearly. He was a superb example of a vitally engaged person who managed to embrace the modest, peaceful life. Yet as a Jewish German during World War II, peace was not then an option for him. Einstein had great fortune in that foreign armies were available and willing to violently defeat an existential threat, from within his own country, to Einstein's modest desires.

***

16

England's greatest playwright noted that our achievements are behind us. Passive memories – remnants of times past – can yield some contentment. But a more active feeling of joy comes from anticipating success in *new* adventures:

Things won are done; joy's soul lies in the doing. – Shakespeare

A business titan once observed that success requires activity, including mistakes:

Success seems to be connected with action. Successful people keep moving. They make mistakes, but they don't quit. – Conrad Hilton

Psychology professor Angela Duckworth has shown that perseverance and passion are overwhelmingly dominant characteristics of successful people. Talent, intelligence, and luck play a part – but successful people are not always gifted, brilliant, or fortunate. In her superb book *Grit*, Prof. Duckworth shows that the most common attributes of high achievers – of winners – involve their passionate interest in a long-term goal and a ferocious determination to pursue it. Their short-term goals fit coherently with that larger goal. They pursue these goals for decades, day-in and day-out, with discipline, willfulness, stamina, and resilience. In short, Prof. Duckworth shows that *sustained, steady effort* is the most critical, universal component of success.

As much as talent counts, effort counts twice… Hidden behind every effortless performance are hours and hours of challenging, effortful, mistake-ridden practice. Trying to do things you can't do, feeling frustrated, failing, fighting the urge to quit, and learning what you need to do differently is <u>exactly</u> the way experts practice.

— Prof. Angela Duckworth, author of *Grit*

The good news is that exertion and diligence are far more within our control than the other contributors to success. Talent is not destiny. People with "grit" have devotional qualities like fortitude, and they work even harder after repeated failures. Studies show that grit is the leading predictor of success. And there's more good news: Prof. Duckworth's book *Grit* shows, in very accessible language, how each of us can cultivate and develop the characteristics and habits of high achievers.

Winning usually brings a temporary form of happiness. Lest we think that winning finally leads us to the bank, a promised land, or heavenly bliss, there's a strong argument that happiness is *not* a destination. It's *not* gained by crossing a goal line. It's *not* a glorious and stable lack of pain, effort, or sorrow. Happiness is more like a practice, or a way of being. It is a feeling of being capable and effective, of having some control, with confidence to meet and overcome adversity. It's an active yet imperfect sense of more fully using our powers to feed healthy appetites and do worthy tasks.

In the great chase for happiness that pervades much of today's thinking, it has come to be understood as a destination. ... But in fact, happiness (however you define it) is a temporary state... Millions of people are doing their best to get to a destination that doesn't exist, at least not in the form they imagine.... [This faulty concept] dooms us to endless comparing of our ordinary selves to someone else's extraordinary, perfect social media moment. ... the many things I tried eventually brought me to a different understanding of what to expect of life.

– Dr. Odelya Gertel Kraybill, trauma therapist

One more twist in our understanding might win back an *active role for peacemaking* in a fulfilled life:

18

Humanity has been grappling with the concept of peace since the dawn of history. When we think of peace today, certain ideas come to mind: A setting uncluttered by noise, a region free of violence, or perhaps a home where family members stop the bickering. These images are striking in that they emphasize something that isn't there: conflict, war, tension, sounds, commotion. But peace is more than a lack of something. It is also a greeting (Peace be with you) and a benediction (Go now in peace) and a gift (Peace I leave with you). What if peace is not an absence, but a presence?

– Dr. Lynda Hassler

Living Authentically, with Rich Connections to Others

When life nears its end, the dying usually do NOT intensely regret their mistaken actions. They more commonly regret their passive omissions – the things they *failed to do*. Palliative care specialist Bronnie Ware has interviewed people who in illness or old age were thinking about their mortality. She found five most common themes of their regrets, expressed here as what they *should have done*.

1. Live true to personal dreams (rather than doing what others expect)
2. Prioritize family (over income)
3. Express true feelings (vs. suppressing them to keep peace)
4. Nourish friendships (instead of neglecting them)
5. Grasp for what truly gratifies (vs. pretending to be contented).

Three of these priorities involve authenticity – (1) true wishes, (3) true feelings, and (5) true gratification. The others emphasize the value of rich connections with family (2) and friends (4). Ware elaborates on these in her compelling, life-giving book entitled *Top Five Regrets Of The Dying*.

One astute journalist has reduced "authenticity" to a simple guideline like Ware's first principle: be true to *your own* priorities and wishes.

The best way to live the life you want to live is to stop worrying about what other people think. — *Jeff Haden*

An irony here is that the people we love and cherish are our ground zero for living fully. Of course their opinions and needs matter. Of course we want to please them. But as the dying see clearly, we should think twice about submitting to others' opinions on how to live. As Shakespeare said:

This above all: to thine own self be true. — Polonius, from *Hamlet*

So, is *active happiness* the right goal? One thoughtful young widow has reflected wisely on raising her daughter, who was only 8 months old when her father died:

I used to think, 'I want to be happy all the time' or 'I want to raise a happy kid.' Now I really want to have meaning in my life and I really want to raise a resilient kid. — Dr. Lucy Kalanithi

Even to our last breaths, humans have a bias toward action. The happiest among us tilt toward living authentically, purposefully, *meaningfully*.

For the English minister, logician, and hymn writer Isaac Watts, living purposefully meant forsaking rest or diversion. Watts says we should fully use our time to pursue our destination(s) and worthy goal(s):

Do not spend the day in gathering flowers by the way side, lest night come upon you before you arrive at your journey's end, and then you will not reach it. — Isaac Watts, in *Logic: The Right Use of Reason*

Yet we're repeatedly advised in our go-go culture to "stop and smell the roses" – to find meaning in the beauty that's readily at hand. As a great artist has observed, some of us are so preoccupied with our treadmill that we ignore beauty that's right in front of us:

There are always flowers for those who want to see them.
– Henri Matisse

Achievement and appreciating beauty are both meaningful choices. Yet our actions often reflect little or no choice at all. Instead we live within a cloud of assumptions and expectations about what we *should be* doing, dominated by habits in what we *are* doing. It can be tragic when authentic choices are postponed until eventually we lack the time, energy, or wellbeing to choose differently. Whatever the past may have been, most of us are fortunate still to have the ability and the time – NOW – to make authentic decisions, living by our own choices rather than someone else's.

Enterprise & Creativity: Risk, Loss, & Daring Greatly

Capitalism is a way to organize action, to incentivize enterprising behavior. It structures up-front payments for the expenses of discovery and invention, of expansion and improvement. A good arts community also includes a system of people and resources to support creators whose works elevate the human spirit. All who rely on such support systems – entrepreneurs, artists, discoverers, and inventors – are known to color "outside the box" from time to time, if not every day. They engage the world beyond normal boundaries.

Creativity of course requires inspiration *and* sheer grunt. Experience teaches that many creations and innovations will be stillborn or eventually fail, as are most of nature's evolutionary experiments with biological variety. Stress and failure are the normal companions of invention and venturing: we simply must manage them when facing the unknown and creating the future.

Venture investors know that an entrepreneur who <u>hasn't</u> failed must have very limited experience with risk. (S)he hasn't ventured "outside the box" enough to make the box blow up. A popular author and speaker well capsulized this perennial truth of business and life:

> *When we make the choice to dare greatly, we sign up to get our asses kicked. We can choose courage or we can choose comfort, but we can't have both. Not at the same time.* – Brené Brown

Within our boxes, experience reduces risk, and habits improve efficiency. We cherish accumulated knowledge and other cornerstones of stability, which make our lives less tumultuous. Reflexively rejecting hard-earned lessons of the past reflects a dangerous mix of arrogance and ignorance. Yet in straying from 'the beaten path' to find better paths, comfortable routines can inhibit fresh ideas and practices. Experience and knowledge can be the anvils against which we hammer the future into being: we honor yet enlarge our experience, strengthen or change habits, cherish old facts and create new ones. Sometimes we discard bad habits and practices. If we're really vigorous we can overturn 'what we know for sure that just ain't so.'

Experienced innovators do not expect a risky adventure to be orderly:

> *Stress and conflict are signs of energy productively engaged.*
>
> –Holman Jenkins Jr., journalist

Creative destruction makes even the winners nervous. It's a natural human instinct to seek shelter from turmoil, working to control our circumstances and shape our future. Shelter shields us from pain. But the real winners are those who embrace the whirlwind, enduring pain to create the future. Whether we conquer, change, or come up short, being challenged is a vital source of meaning. We triumph by facing fear rather than yielding to it:

To put meaning in one's life may end in madness,
But life without meaning is the torture
Of restlessness and vague desire—
It is a boat longing for the sea and yet afraid.

—Edgar Lee Masters, *Spoon River Anthology*

So is it possible for voyagers and activists, artists, and entrepreneurs, to be really *happy* amid all their fear and struggle? Sages and psychologists seem to say yes IF happiness is tied to hopeful striving. They seem to say no if happiness is understood as passive contentment.

This aligns with the stereotype of the "tormented artist," creatively striving in the face of anguish. However, my first-hand experience has shown that well-adjusted people can also be creative and enterprising. Their "well-adjustedness" usually involves a balance between striving and accepting:

If you can meet with Triumph and Disaster
And treat those two impostors just the same...
Yours is the Earth and everything that's in it.
– from IF, by Rudyard Kipling

Acceptance is vital when striving won't change an outcome. It plays a key role also after a failure or loss. Given a life-threatening diagnosis, a young professor beautifully expressed her acceptance with this gem in four words:

Surrender is not weakness.   – Kate Bowler

Shakespeare used three times as many words to make a similar point:

Things without all remedy should be without regard.
What's done is done.   – Shakespeare

Determining exactly *when* striving becomes futile is no easy distinction. Cancer victims often "fight" to the very end, enduring great suffering from poisons, burning and cutting (i.e., chemotherapy, radiation, and surgery). Cancer treatments often deliver only marginally extended life, though some margins are growing longer and many cure rates are increasing.

Losses or failures sometimes occur in slow motion, as chances for escape steadily diminish. Think of a losing ballgame, as the clock winds down and yet another scoring opportunity is missed. Think of a failing business, as managers repeatedly try new strategies or tactics to revive it. Business students are taught how to manage "sunk costs" as prospects dim. This is essentially a fancy concept for not crying over spilled milk. It is a refusal to put good money after bad. It means facing the future *anew*.

We might notice another embedded lesson in these examples – that after failure or tragedy, we must *move on*. Time and resources are wasted by trying to rescue the past – except that new interpretations can change how we *understand* history. New viewpoints can how we might better *manage* today and tomorrow. The only changeable things about the past are how we describe, explain, and act on it.

In focusing our attention on things nearby and ahead, another key step is to be more conscious of *what we can influence or control*. One blogger struggled mightily for control during the pandemic of 2020 before adopting a three-tiered model for his attention:

> *[I read] that there are only three types of business in the world; my business, your business and God's business. This past year has taught me to live in my business and avoid spending time in the other two. They only lead to suffering.*   – Chris Mamula

***

24

Years ago I was invited to a presentation on "the universal human experience." Chatter among attendees produced a lot of guesses – *love, work, sleep* – or maybe *death*? How about *sex*? Another good guess would have been *struggle*. But none of us correctly anticipated *loss*.

The speaker's husband had died suddenly, soon after moving to a new city with a newborn baby. Rather than dwell on her lone tragedy, she told her story as a personal version of a universal experience: loss. As sages have observed, time destroys all things, including health and ultimately life itself.

While dying prematurely from lung cancer, Dr. Paul Kalanithi – Lucy's husband – wrote to their infant daughter with grace, wisdom, and foresight. Anticipating her future distress, he shared with Cady his profound acceptance of the circumstances her birth had shaped:

> *Do not, I pray, discount that you filled the dying man's days with a joy unknown to me in all my prior years. A joy that does not hunger for more and more, but rests, satisfied. In this time, right now, that is an enormous thing.* – Paul Kalanithi, *When Breath Becomes Air*

Kalanithi's book, *When Breath Becomes Air*, is filled with courage, beauty, elegance, and humor amid his decline to an early end. His wisdom is a model to emulate. Paul's widow Lucy later taught young Cady a verse of acceptance and defiance, and Cady used it to sing herself to sleep:

> *I don't have to be perfect, I just have to be brave.*
> – Cady Kalanithi

We'd do well to calibrate our balance between resisting and accepting losses, embracing or relinquishing joy. It will be a blessing to find that balance again and again, skillfully and gracefully, especially as our own final loss becomes imminent.

Fear and Control

Evolution has exquisitely tuned our attention and that of all other creatures. We notice threats above all else.

Failing to notice a hungry tiger's erect tail in a golden field of wheat will substantially lower the probability you'll pass genes to future generations. So fear and vulnerability are two of our most powerful motivators. They're probably more potent even than greed and ambition. Many conflicts are ultimately about fear – of alien political values, of authority in the wrong hands, of weak control over important circumstances.

Untamed fear is a towering obstacle to peace of mind. It's a robust source of stress and struggle. How can we manage our worries and fears well enough to escape the storm – or even better, to engage and tame it?

It's easy to overlook our power to cope with things through adaptation, the central mechanism of evolutionary survival. Adaptation works especially well over long time periods: it has a track record of several million years. For a time in the 1970s it was fashionable to fret that modern high-consumption economies would produce so much trash that we would eventually bury ourselves under it. I was relieved and grateful then to find a historian's article explaining that for eons, humans have been burying their trash and living on top of it. When archaeologists excavate old cities, they routinely find sequential layers of civilization. Street levels in major cities today are many feet higher than they were centuries ago. Shellfish layers are now limestone in many places... and so on and on. The idea that humans *cannot* adapt to debris is absurd, a modern version of Chicken Little's declaration that the sky is falling. Yet at one time not so long ago, fear of rampant garbage was a hand-wringer.

Horse manure was once a major health hazard in cities, then the automobile was invented. Many people complain about today's Styrofoam and plastic packaging, which causes real problems – but minor ones compared to history's tons of rotting food. The presence of so much rot in cities required trash to be efficiently and timely disposed to avoid serious infectious illness. Modern packaging and refrigeration have eliminated huge amounts of waste and disease, enabling ever larger, healthier populations. But we hear mostly about the problems of packaging waste.

The Chicken Little style of predicting doom is a long and storied tradition. Yet doomsayers regularly fail to account for human adaptability, ingenuity, and innovation. Be not afraid. Or at least seek a sense of context that confines fears within reasonable boundaries.

The point here is that the human intellect is our greatest resource – more than any material asset. We don't appear to be anywhere near exhausting our inventions and discoveries. Many brilliant people are now working to replicate, extend, and multiply our mental powers in the form of artificial intelligence. But like clockwork we're treated to scary AI stories warning that silicon-based intelligence might take our jobs or make carbon-based (i.e. human) intelligence obsolete. Such stories can look like an imaginary tiger's tail in a promising field of wheat. When tempted to jump off the dizzying carousel of striving, a little digging can restore perspective, and bury scarecrows that disturb our peace of mind. But that alone isn't enough.

Surprise! politicians, entertainers, and media figures have figured out that conflicts and threats magnetically draw our attention. There's a cynical slogan among media types about the top daily news story:

If it bleeds, it leads.

That's a steady diet that media offers. For businesses whose success depends on their numbers of followers (whether readers, viewers, a theater's "butts in seats," or online "eyeballs"), gaining and keeping audience attention is *everything*. So demands for your attention are likely to include a lot of scary or disturbing stories and controversies.

The Nobel-winning economist Daniel Kahneman notes that one of our greatest reasons for misjudging probabilities – and scaring ourselves in the process – is that *we don't know the base rates* for most occurrences. We respond to emotions stirred by a vivid fear, not statistical facts (e.g., that sharks rarely attack humans and people rarely win lotteries). This is called the "availability heuristic" – a problem-solving shortcut that our brains use. Our intuition grabs for the most available comparable example, like a scary story we heard recently. So we end up worrying about many things that are exceedingly unlikely to touch us personally (like terrorism or airplane crashes). We're blasé about the risks that are far more likely to really hurt us, like falls at home (especially from a ladder), vehicle crashes (including bicycles), and chronic but preventable diseases (whose destruction creeps up on us gradually). An inflaming story on the news is highly "available" for a time... but it's not necessarily a signal that we're doomed or saved. First and foremost it's a signal chosen by others to get and keep our attention.

Speaking of the world going to hell, which is announced regularly by headlines about *the death of* this or *the crisis of* that, several authors have shown convincingly that the world is rapidly getting better, even as real threats remain ever-present. Greg Easterbrook's *Progress Paradox* and *It's Better Than It Looks* explore why we feel so bad when things are improving so much. Charles Kenny's *Getting Better* celebrates global development in our era of unprecedented human development. *Abundance*, by Peter Diamandis and Steven Kotler, glimpses a future that's "better than you think" because scientists, entrepreneurs and investors are driving a dramatic

28

wave of innovation. Steven Pinker, in two books entitled *The Better Angels of Our Nature* and *Enlightenment Now*, digests massive data sets to show how the world is dramatically improving on four separate time scales (beginning with feudalism, the Enlightenment, the onset of Industrialization, or the mid-20th century). Pinker points out that good-news stories develop so slowly that they're missed in the urgencies of the daily news cycle:

> *Bad things can happen quickly, but good things aren't built in a day, and as they unfold, they will be out of sync with the news cycle. The peace researcher Johan Galtung pointed out that if a newspaper came out once every 50 years, it would not report half a century of celebrity gossip and political scandals. It would report momentous global changes such as the increase in life expectancy. – Steven Pinker*

Election year coverage is especially likely to feature some crisis or another. And voila, you can address that crisis by voting for Candidate Jones:

> *The whole aim of practical politics is to keep the populace alarmed (and hence clamorous to be led to safety) by menacing it with an endless series of hobgoblins, all of them imaginary. –* H.L. Mencken

Mencken goes too far in saying all the hobgoblins are imaginary. It's not that the issues are fake – they're just predictably exaggerated by candidates who need voter turnout, or editors who need readers. Think of losing the space race to the Soviets' Sputnik in 1960. Death by Goldwater's nuclear trigger-finger in 1964. 1988's Willie Horton ad about a furloughed prisoner's crime, hinting at imminent chaos in the streets if an opponent is elected. Occupy Wall Street (and domination by the 1%) in 2016. Black Lives Matter, urban violence, and progressive warnings in 2020 of environmental cataclysm. And plenty in between.

Count on it: things we fear or resent will surge to the forefront every election cycle, like returning comets. The weeks before a big election are a good time to remind ourselves that the heavens remain... that the sun is extremely likely to keep appearing daily for the indefinite future. And that half of our countrymen don't have to be enemies for elections to function.

Just two months after 2020's tumultuous elections, a former Starbucks executive rented an RV to travel with his son through America's Pacific Northwest region. Unlike the hostile agitation portrayed daily in the media, these travelers encountered helpful people going about their daily lives, offering kind favors. They heard contented, unhurried conversation about the enduring things like "family, home, and what brought us out their way:"

Our view of our fellow Americans has been distorted by social media and the news, which relentlessly focus on the most disruptive and negative forces in our country. But ordinary, generous people like the ones my son and I met make up most of America—the populous majority that doesn't feed on online grievances. Most of the country is too busy living. As I handed the keys back to the owner of the [rented] RV, I told him that I felt as if I had rediscovered my country... A wide, proud smile came over his face. In broken English, this Chinese software engineer, originally from Shenzhen, replied "Of course! That's why I rent out my RV . . . so Americans can see how beautiful America is!

– John Kelly

Worry

Worry is a close cousin to fear. We struggle mightily with both. Samuel Clemens (pen-named Mark Twain) cleverly described a common experience of worry:

> *I am an old man and have known a great many troubles, but most of them never happened.*
>
> – Mark Twain (also attributed to Michel Montaigne)

A first-century Stoic and Roman statesman was well aware of our tendency to envision rampant threats:

> *There are more things... likely to frighten us than there are to crush us; we suffer more often in imagination than in reality.*
>
> – Seneca

A 20th century economist once joked about his profession's pessimism, which led to a dismal, anxiety-producing record in economic predictions:

> *Declines in U.S. stock prices have predicted nine of the last five recessions.* – Paul Samuelson, economics Nobelist

Some fears are highly justified – our problems and shortcomings are real. But we seem to have a have a hard time calibrating our threat assessment, and our emotional responses to them. As we saw with judging risk, we *accept and adapt* to certain fears (like dying from a traffic accident) yet we struggle exhaustively with others (like bad election outcomes).

A fine definition of courage is to have *presence of mind and bias to action*. These are the basic mechanisms of facing the vivid obstacles in our many fears, threats, risks, or vulnerabilities. Economist Daniel Kahneman, who urges us to learn the base rates of common risks, has defined courage as involving <u>measured</u> risk rather than braving the wild unknown:

Courage is willingness to take the risk once you know the odds. Optimistic overconfidence means you are taking the risk because you don't know the odds. It's a big difference.   – Daniel Kahneman

Caution has its place, of course. As Shakespeare wrote in *Henry IV*: *"the better part of valor is discretion."* My dear friend Chris penned a similarly cautious but witty remark on a Post-it note in his home. He was responding to an inspirational question his wife had framed for a daughter's bedroom.

(Framed inspiration): *What if... you traded fear for curiosity?*
(Post-it addendum): *If a grizzly bear were nearby, it would be a bad trade.*

I live for wit like that. But rampant scare stories used in media, advertising, and especially politics are no laughing matter. Fortunately, we can benefit from the proverb that *"a tactic perceived is no tactic at all."* When I detect someone trying to frighten or intimidate me, I think of *The Wizard of Oz*. Dorothy, with knees quivering, is overwhelmed by the great, powerful Oz, of booming voice and ghostly image. Then her little dog Toto pulls back a curtain, revealing a stammering little man exposed for who he really is.

It's worth thinking about which of our big fears may be induced by people for their benefit. It's vital to see how so many fears are over-magnified by our fearful imaginations and instincts. Finding the *real* tiger's tail in that field of wheat is a challenge more likely to be conquered with calm reason.

Polarization & Protest

America is, politically speaking, a 52/48 nation (sometimes 51/49 or 50/50). Only a rare candidate or issue gains 60+% support. It's nearly impossible for some 200 million voters to agree on much of anything. And it's absurd to think that 48% are utterly, completely wrong on any specific choice.

Other electoral democracies have similar records, swinging on narrow margins between hugely different views and ideologies. Some describe this pattern as "bouncing between guardrails." Increasingly expensive, exhausting elections determine which side will grab the steering wheel for the coming years. Both sides worry that a guardrail will break, failing to protect the political objectives they hold dear. Meanwhile, each side works diligently to dismantle an opposing guardrail that obstructs their dreams.

Along with this come protests (peaceful or not), disruption, criticism, aggression, debates about the use of force, snark, derision, and more. Factions undermine and degrade one another, and then one almost always pleads for unity after winning an election. Victors imagine peace on their own terms. Democracy (more specifically, a representative republic) contests political visions with rowdy and noisy vigor, signifying energy and health. Quiet, polite contests reflect disinterest or lethargy, little or no diversity, or maybe that the stakes are not very high. (Now there's an idea – elections with less at stake!).

So how much rowdiness is too much? Can we get off this spinning wheel, or at least slow it down? Aren't the divisive issues too big to ignore?

Peace can be easily achieved: simply accept your opponent's terms. But it can't be surprising that few losing factions appear ready to resign the contest, even as winners suddenly find new respect for civility and unity in doing things their way. One cultural observer cites a clever aphorism that shows why political struggle is never-ending:

There are no lost causes, because there are no gained causes.
– W.R. Inge, derived from T.S. Eliot

This view is more generally phrased by a skeptical novelist:

Never think you've seen the last of anything. – Eudora Welty

Considering today's common view that polarization is worse than ever, one historian notes that an overreaching winner plants the seeds of future defeat:

Americans hate one thing more than a sore loser, and that is an arrogant, vindictive – and bullying – winner. – Victor Davis Hanson

Tyranny and domination, external and internal, are enemies of free people. The founding documents of the U.S. say as much. Winston Churchill's words for Great Britain in 1940 applied just as well to Ukraine in 2022, where a courageous leader inspired his country to repudiate and defeat an attempt to dominate them:

Nations that go down fighting rise again, but those who surrender tamely are finished... If this long island story of ours is to end at last, let it end only when each one of us lies choking in his own blood upon the ground.   – *Winston Churchill*

To a critic who demanded to know how much defense is enough, Churchill responded "*embalm, cremate, bury at sea, take no chances*" (presumably for the enemy, if not the critic). The animating contest endures, thankfully. We turn a corner to find another corner. Around a bend is another bend.

Suppressing Tyranny vs. Forming a Perfect Union

In their great wisdom, a top priority for America's founders was to *suppress tyranny*. Submitting to a tyrant certainly would be one way to end our enduring contests of values, principles and opinions. We should constantly remember the good news that the U.S. Constitution was brilliantly structured to balance opposing forces, to check their excesses, and to require opponents to engage each other if they hope to get anything done.

America's founders knew there is no 'happily ever after.' Their ultimate priority was to ensure that no faction can permanently prevail. In *Federalist No. 10*, James Madison brilliantly expressed how an ongoing competition of varied interests is <u>inevitable</u> among fallible, free people:

> *As long as the reason of man continues fallible, and he is at liberty to exercise it, different opinions will be formed. [This diversity is] an insuperable obstacle to an uniformity of interests. The protection of these faculties is the first object of government. From the protection of different and unequal faculties of acquiring property, the possession of different degrees and kinds of property immediately results: And from the influence of these on the sentiments and views of the respective proprietors, ensues a division of the society into different interests and parties. The latent causes of faction are thus sown in the nature of man…. Liberty is to faction, what air is to fire, an aliment without which it instantly expires. But it could not be a less folly to abolish liberty, which is essential to political life, because it nourishes faction, than it would be to wish the annihilation of air, which is essential to animal life, because it imparts to fire its destructive agency.*
>
> – James Madison, Federalist No. 10

The word *faction* can sound negative, indicating separation, obstruction, and insensitive self-interest. But a faction is identical to a *caucus* or a *coalition*, which succeeds politically by aggregating lots of votes in many settings and configurations. Consensus is a mighty political force, for good reasons. One of the reasons is that consensus requires collaboration within the constant agitation (if not hostility) of adversary politics.

Politics is a team sport. An alienated politician can have a tough time getting much done. Yet alienation also is a starting point for change. Political reform usually is imposed from without rather than initiated from within. Socio-political change requires building new coalitions, and winning converts to support destabilizing ideas. Demanding "change" and rejecting the status quo are evergreen election themes. They're our mechanisms for getting better (though "change" also can make things worse).

Often change means amplifying a *different* side of dualities like those we're examining here: more peace and less righteous struggle, less diversity and more unity, fewer rules and more reliance on conscience, and many more.

Political diversity produces a ceaselessly confusing kaleidoscope of shifting forces and positions. A call to simplify – and divide – may indicate that tensions are peaking, soon to be followed by a call to war:

> *There are but two parties now, traitors and patriots.*
> – Ulysses S. Grant, 1861, after shots fired on Ft. Sumter
> *You're either with us or against us in the fight against terror.*
> – George W. Bush, 2001, after World Trade Center attacks

Here's a salute to confused, messy politics. Hardened division can be far more destructive than the rowdy grind.

This discussion of peace vs. striving is not the place to fully develop political theories. Nor is it the place to assess the details of constitutional governance and its many subtleties. But we might note that the *bigger* the stakes are, and the more *centralized and universal* the proposed solution may be, the *nastier* the fight, and the harder it is to peacefully co-exist. One legal scholar, a specialist in the administrative state, traces the U.S. trend toward centralization to U.S. Supreme Court decisions that supported more

36

regulatory power within the U.S. Congress. So many matters once left to the states now are delegated to executive branch administrators:

> *In recent decades, the federal government has relied on the court's expansive vision of its legislative power to regulate education, speech, healthcare, insurance, sexual relations, and other areas that once seemed largely beyond Washington's reach... Presidential elections therefore elicit an intensity of feeling that strains lawful, let alone civilized, conduct. They have become do-or-die battles for control of massive regulatory power. With so much riding on a single election, the stakes become too high. An almost irresistible incentive exists to suppress opponents and their views—abandoning all traditions of cooperation, tolerance and freedom of speech. There also are heightened incentives for dishonesty and corruption—as well as intensified fears about such things... In the resulting all-or-nothing battles, politics becomes warfare.... Our high court might have been content with making federal regulation highly expansive. Or in making it highly administrative. Instead, it did both, structurally ensuring that presidential conflicts will tear the nation apart.*
>
> – Philip Hamburger, CEO, New Civil Liberties Alliance

There's little escape from a universal solution imposed by the other guy, especially if (s)he's an unelected administrator. So the fight becomes more intense, even desperate. One-size-fits-all blends our differences toward uniformity; it enables vast mistakes by people who think there's one right answer (which of course is *their* answer). A path to less conflict might be *less* insistence that one size fits all. That would mean *more* liberty, greater tolerance for differing opinions and styles, and more acceptance of variety among states, cities, countries, and other jurisdictions.

We might lower our expectation that national governments and courts should (or even *can*) resolve our every dispute, producing some glorious ideal. Fifty brush fires might be more controllable than one forest fire. More widely distributed fires surely lower the risk of a conflagration.

> *Government is not reason or eloquence, it is force. Like fire, it is a dangerous servant and a fearful master.*
>
> – political epigram spuriously attributed to George Washington

When a national solution is necessary, legislatures are the political branch best organized to force compromises. This is *unlike* decrees from courts, executive orders, and administrative decisions by non-elected regulators. Legislative rules and processes including hearings, motions to amend, supermajority requirements, and filibusters; all of these *obstruct quick action*. They tend to force engagement if not bipartisanship. Calls for quick legislative action, sometimes claiming an emergency is afoot, often mask an attempt to bypass the legislative practices that support collaboration and suppress tyranny. Shoot, ready, aim is a bad sequence.

Meanwhile, we're protected by certain judicial traditions such as adopting the least intrusive remedies, making incremental rather than radical change, and deferring to representative branches of government. Each of these cautious principles avoid the whipsaw effects that landmark decisions can produce in polarized, divided government. They tilt decision-making toward individuals or their elected representatives rather than brilliant lawyers, judges, administrators, and scientists.

Modesty in the courts, and in the other branches of government, preserve their institutional stability, dignity, and authority. These are the foundations of continued respect and reliable enforcement of future decisions.

Fight or Flight

We have choices. We engage or retreat, act reflexively or deliberately, and use hostile or respectful manners as we seek to conquer or collaborate.

Many people are quick to air grievances and mock others, especially via social media. One columnist captured how all the harsh rhetoric produces distaste, contempt, and exhaustion:

There is one certainty in American life that you can take to the bank: the polarization of politics... There's no way to turn off the daily artillery barrages of political war, from the nation's leadership to citizens intensely piling bile and mockery into websites and social-media platforms. [Unlike the coronavirus], this is the virus that won't stop killing the country. – Daniel Henninger, journalist

As of this writing, the U.S. is not yet killed. But Henninger's overstatement about "killing the country" is a vivid way to bemoan the hostility that drones on among 'we the people.' Consider how two opposing political leaders set the tone in their time, including an astounding claim that being civil to opponents is a weakness, and that strength is shown by *in*civility:

[2016]: You know, to just be grossly generalistic, you could put half of Trump's supporters into what I call the basket of deplorables. Right? The racist, sexist, homophobic, xenophobic, Islamaphobic — you name it... [2018]: You cannot be civil with a political party that wants to destroy what you stand for, what you care about. That's why I believe, if we are fortunate enough to win back the House and or the Senate, that's when civility can start again. But until then, the only thing that the Republicans seem to recognize and respect is strength. – Hillary Clinton

Such thinking is symmetric: it's held to a degree by radicalized members of every party or faction. It's a formula for having *at most* about half of the country behaving with civility or respect at any given time. Strength in adversity is a good formula to avoid being run over (as in *"peace through strength"*). But one wonders which uncivil behaviors are supposed to be included in this kind of "strength" – and which are beyond the pale.

Meanwhile, Clinton's nemesis Donald Trump wasn't known for grace, tact, deference, or respecting norms. Predictably, he's been hated or loved for it:

Sleepy Creepy Joe Biden... Crazy Bernie Sanders... Crooked Hillary... Goofy Elizabeth Warren, sometimes referred to as Pocahontas because she faked the fact she is native American, is a lowlife!...a stone-cold phony named Robert Francis O'Rourke, sometimes referred to as 'Beto.'... Lightweight Senator Kirsten Gillibrand, a total flunky for Chuck Schumer... Mini Mike Bloomberg... Shifty Schiff... Low-IQ Maxine Waters... Gretchen Half-Whitmer... Senator Joe Munchkin... Al Franken[stein]... Cryin' Chuck Schumer... Fat Jerry Nadler... Evita Ocasio-Cortez... RINO Romney... Loser McCain... Little Marco... Low energy Jeb... 1-for-38 Kasich... Zero chance Fiorina... Jeff Flakey... Leakin' James Comey... – Donald Trump, 2015-2020, mostly via Twitter

Trash talk, rudeness, and contempt are often barely disguised in social media. A tweeter's capsulized self-description – a mini-profile – frequently announces that (s)he is "proud" of some personal characteristic or status. New Jersey Gov. Phil Murphy has said he is proud to be a husband and father, proud to lead New Jersey... and then (pridefully?) blasts a member of the opposing political party for millions to see:

40

It is also beyond the pale that Rep Matt Putz – I mean @RepMattGaetz – would participate in this. What a fool. Matt – You are not welcome in New Jersey, and frankly I don't ever want you back in this state.   – @GovMurphy

Such snarling contempt is broadcast instantly, worldwide. It goes far beyond responding to one offender. The key audience here is the hordes of spectators; a fighting message goes to thousands or millions of voluntary voyeurs, called followers. From anywhere in the world, followers can now become outraged over somebody else's fight. That's the point – to galvanize the herd with political loyalty or action. Sending such divisive comments to a single person only would hardly be worth the effort.

[In this category of "things aren't always what they seem," consider the opposite case: a bumper sticker saying "My kid is an honor student at Smith School." Displayed to many, the message mostly benefits the student.]

In the mid-twentieth century, young Arthur Ashe's father explicitly advised him against contempt, though he had every excuse to be angry. Arthur came to be a mild-mannered, dignified tennis pro, widely respected as a black-skinned champion in a class-dominated, white-skinned sport. Arthur achieved in part because he remembered his father's advice:

You don't get nowhere by making enemies. You gain by helping others.
      – Arthur Ashe Sr.

Journalist Peggy Noonan has well captured the *tactical* nature of polarized, disrespectful, angry and disruptive political behavior. Her observations apply across the political spectrum, to radicalized factions on both sides. In 2020 she responded specifically to the polarizing actions of young renegades energizing the Left:

None of this is a misfortune of temperament. It is a strategy and it is working. Polarization yields prominence. The new lefties equate peacefulness with complacency... There is always a great temptation among the young in politics, and especially of the left, to see common respect as an admission of insincerity in opposing injustice. If you were sincere you'd be passionate—fierce and rude... They believe that to be enraged is to demonstrate seriousness... You must be crude to show the authenticity of your contempt for injustice.

– Peggy Noonan, 2020

Journalist George Will has noted a similar fierceness among some supporters of Donald Trump on the right. Will puts political anger from both sides in yet another perspective:

There's a small number of Americans who only feel alive when they're angry. I don't think most Americans are angry. I think they're exhausted and they are longing for a restoration of normality... Most Americans are raising children, going on with their lives... Someone is going to come along in either party and say, 'Deep breath, America, calm down, we are not enemies, we must not be enemies,' to take a line from Lincoln's great first inaugural address.

– George Will, 2022

More than 1½ centuries ago, Lincoln's First Inaugural Address appealed to the "better angels of our nature:"

We are not enemies, but friends. We must not be enemies. Though passion may have strained it must not break our bonds of affection. The mystic chords of memory, stretching from every battlefield and patriot grave to every living heart and hearthstone all over this broad land, will yet swell the chorus of the Union, when again touched, as surely they will be, by the better angels of our nature.

– Abraham Lincoln, 1861

In the mid-twentieth century, Dale Carnegie built a large seminar and publishing business following the success of his 1936 book, *How to Win Friends and Influence People.* This flagship title sold 30 million copies over decades, beginning at a time when America's population was only about 130 million people. A typical Carnegie lesson echoed a Lincoln proverb: *'you can catch more flies with honey than with vinegar.'*

Common wisdom, then and now, says that harsh remarks persuade nobody. They usually cause adversaries to dig in their heels. Any salesman can tell you that treating prospective buyers with bile and spit will never persuade them. But a contemptuous performance might please onlookers, especially those eager to despise and discredit an "enemy" camp.

Technology increasingly bridges large distances. It connects people who don't know one another very well. Tech amplifies opinions among strangers who've had little or no opportunity to build mutual respect. Such strangers also have little or no need to minimize alienation, because social media provides few opportunities to build the deeper relationships that preserve a common future. Today's dramatic spectacle of condescension and conflict is enlarged by our physical separation. Distance obliterates the potential for delicate, tentative interplay among people whose in-person decency might produce some mutual respect, trust, and reconciliation.

When we're electronically mediated, triumphant political declarations multiply, cheered on by like-minded geese flying in formation. These flocks are hostile to opponents *and* to any ally who shows signs of defecting or compromising. Splashy spectacles are replayed by news sites, exciting readers with click bait under headlines about who "ripped," "blasted," "slammed" or "schooled" the enemy. The "news" reports on various squabbles *about* events, secondary to the events themselves. This new type of 'bleeding lead' is catnip for media viewers in the Internet era. Butts migrate to seats, and eyeballs to screens, to enjoy the blood-sport spectacle.

It's worth noting here that political controversies powerfully *enter the experience* of people who identify as victims of injustice. Feeling aggrieved, convinced that you're harmed or violated, is not a promising way to develop a calm, patient approach to managing conflicts. Our victim-oriented culture, with competitive debates over who is most damaged, provides grand opportunities for politicians to declare unbounded commitment to right society's wrongs. The wrongs may be real or imagined; all are likely to be highly magnified by power-seeking saviors.

An insulting, demeaning style can make a speaker look righteous and bold. It also can make them look small and miserable, like the Wizard of Oz. Yet experience shows that a more accurate word for an agitated political crusader is often "winner," after voters reward such behavior.

Here we have a great question of human nature: if we want results from others, how should we treat them? Whether in public and private, whether among friends or opponents – is collaborating or encouraging others as effective as denouncing and disrespecting them?

Steve Jobs was enormously successful as the driving spirit of Apple, maker of innovative computers, iPhones, iPads and so much more. During his early career he famously was harsh, abrasive, and obnoxious. He often delivered a short, simple judgment: "that sucks." Over time his style smoothed, giving colleagues and employees heavy doses of inspiration to tackle monumentally hard tasks. Jobs pushed people beyond what they thought their limits to be, and together they succeeded wildly. His success was so huge that later Silicon Valley leaders have debated whether success requires them also to be assholes. It's so much easier than being inspirational.

The quirky abrasiveness of the young Jobs could be seen as a light version of the style advised by Niccolò Machiavelli, an Italian diplomat and writer during the violent Middle Ages. Machiavelli's 1513 work, *The Prince,* said that a ruler is better off being widely feared rather than greatly loved. In further remarks (about *public* life, making them far less relevant to Jobs' example in business), Machiavelli advised that public and private morality are very different because getting or keeping state power requires deceit, treachery, and even violent force to suppress or eliminate political rivals and popular resistance. The term "Machiavellian" has come to mean "ruthless." Machiavelli's teachings are categorized as political "realism," in bright contrast with dreamy, cheery views about how political goals are achieved. An American novelist (and Nobel winner) said a bare-knuckle pattern is seen broadly in American history and culture:

It has always seemed strange to me... the things we admire in men, kindness and generosity, openness, honesty, understanding and feeling, are the concomitants of failure in our system. And those traits we detest, sharpness, greed, acquisitiveness, meanness, egotism and self-interest, are the traits of success. And while men admire the quality of the first they love the produce of the second."
                                                                    – John Steinbeck

Long after Machiavelli, there lived another 20th-century "realist," the American community activist Saul Alinsky. His 1971 book *Rules For Radicals* is admired and feared as a handbook for provoking political adversaries in the quest for social justice. Consider a few of his rules:

Generally success or failure is a mighty determinant of ethics.... any effective means is automatically judged by the opposition as being unethical... you do what you can with what you have and clothe it in moral arguments.

If the organizer begins with an affirmation of love for people, he promptly turns everyone off. If, on the other hand, he begins with a denunciation of exploiting employers, slum landlords, police shakedowns, gouging merchants, he is inside their experience and they accept him. ...

The organizer dedicated to changing the life of a particular community must first rub raw the resentments [and] fan the latent hostilities of many of the people to the point of overt expression. He must search out controversy and issues, rather than avoid them, for unless there is controversy people are not concerned enough to act.

Power is not only what you have but what the enemy thinks you have.

Never go outside the experience of your people... Wherever possible go outside the experience of the enemy. Here you want to cause confusion, fear, and retreat.

Ridicule is man's most potent weapon.

Pick the target, freeze it, personalize it, and polarize it.
– Saul Alinsky

A similar outlook was expressed by a prickly major league baseball manager:

Nice guys finish last.   – Leo Durocher

Machiavelli, Steinbeck, Alinsky, Durocher and Steve Jobs had little patience for romantic ideals about human behavior. Their observations and techniques are full of strife – and little or no peace.

Trust & Collaboration vs. Suspicion & Punishment

In recent decades psychologists have thoroughly studied a simple game, *The Prisoner's Dilemma*. Two players are rewarded or punished based on their patterns of cooperation or selfishness. Player behavior in this game helps researchers better understand peaceful cooperation and bitter betrayal. It also helps the researchers to speculate on how morality developed through the ages as humans competed and cooperated. The details rules of *The Prisoner's Dilemma* can vary, but generally speaking:

- if both players cooperate, proceeds are split evenly
- If one player defects (betrays cooperation) while the other continues to cooperate, all proceeds go to the defector
- If both players defect, each player receives little or nothing

There's a big payoff for one player if (s)he can betray the other while that opponent naively cooperates. This suggests a strategy of building trust and then betraying it. Many players eventually yield to that temptation.

The Golden Rule of morality ("do unto others as you'd have them do unto you") is a general principle found in every religion. It suggests that optimal outcomes are achieved by consistent, trustful cooperation for mutual benefit. But psychologists have found that consistently collaborating is NOT a winning long-term strategy in *The Prisoner's Dilemma*. Here each player is incentivized to betray as often as (s)he can get away with it. Instead, a strategy of tit-for-tat has been found to optimize results in the long run, for both players. Tit-for-tat means a player simply, consistently makes the same choice that his or her opponent has just made. The certain prospect of punishment minimizes betrayal, and trust never fully develops between the players. Skepticism and retaliation for bad behavior rule the day, especially in large communities. Trust thrives much better in small settings.

Now you know a bit more about why political trust and cooperation are so hard to achieve. And about why Mutually Assured Destruction (MAD) has been a prominent strategy for international armaments.

We might mention also that our belief systems depend heavily on trust. We *think* we've rationally, coolly analyzed things to reach measured judgments. Indeed we may have been independently thoughtful in some cases. But often we've trusted the analysis or judgment of a parent, friend, spouse or other trusted authority. Such trusted people can be a huge key for changing minds. Instead of arguments (*Yes, but…; But what about X…; The difference is…*) persuaders might instead focus over time on being trustworthy – generous, open, kind – even if a bit of tit-for-tat is required for betrayals along the way. Being a warm, trusted friend surely is a better path for creating change than snark and triumphalism. Though events sometimes force change upon us, people are far more likely to be pulled and loved into change rather than pushed or beaten into it. Persuading someone in a loving spirit takes time, just like building trust.

Rather than explore more about the glories and corruptions of human nature, suffice it to say that an active, highly engaged life will encounter many highlifes and lowlifes. Even the most peaceful monk will be exposed to human conflicts and shortcomings, unless all his companions are angels. Grimm's Fairy Tales and Aesop's Fables long ago gave young children quite harsh accounts of reality, with tales of death and predation, including stories of people being eaten. Evil abides, of course – then and now.

But today's world is, in many ways, far less harsh than in the old days. Rather than condemning ourselves to a never-ending tit-for-tat struggle with foe and friend alike, let's take a look at some alternatives based on judicious trust and respect.

Rather Than Fighting: Accept, Abandon, Divert, or Respect

An alternate strategy for managing disagreement is to ***accept opposition*** and ***debate tactfully - insincerely if necessary***. Fiercely opposed U.S. Senators call each other "my good friend," even when they don't seem to mean it. Good manners support constructive bonds between opponents who otherwise may be tempted to go for the throat. Requiring some measure of decorum and implied respect (even if insincere) might seem a small request with little cost. But in demanding that leaders always exhibit good manners and act with dignity, we might overlook at least two factors:

- Anger powerfully motivates, and politicians need motivated followers. Negative political advertising is commonly bemoaned, but 'raising the opponent's negatives' rarely ends for a simple reason: it works. Politicians know that many votes are cast *against* the opposition rather than *for* their own candidate or platform. As political operator Karl Rove has observed: *hostility motivates voters as much as enthusiasm does*.

- Vigorous dispute is a perpetual condition of healthy politics. Remember, stress and conflict are signs of "energy productively engaged." Rhetorical and even physical excesses are no stranger to American history. Describing America's past as "*rough and tumble*" is a polite understatement. For centuries the rowdy toolkit of partisans has included abusive allegations and lawsuits. As one lawyer friend says about the Western legal system, "you could sue the Pope for bastardy." Empty accusations are cheap weapons. Vice President Thomas Jefferson, running against sitting President John Adams in 1800 for the next term,

49

described the Adams administration as *"a reign of witches."* Jefferson's campaign accused Adams of ambiguous sexuality – of being a *"hideous hermaphroditical character, which has neither the force and firmness of a man, nor the gentleness and sensibility of a woman."* Adams' campaign responded by describing Jefferson as *"a mean-spirited, low-lived fellow, the son of a half-breed Indian squaw, sired by a Virginia mulatto father."* Remarkably, in old age Adams and Jefferson became devoted friends and sentimental correspondents despite long-past insults. We remember them as dignified founding fathers, but they could scrap nasty with the best. Their ability over time to form a friendship gives us a story and example to cherish.

In 1856, Rep. Preston Brooks of South Carolina used his walking cane to batter Massachusetts Sen. Charles Sumner nearly to death on the U.S. Senate floor. Sumner had recently spoken as an abolitionistagainst the possibility that a new state, Kansas, might permit slavery. Sumner had said that his opponent, Sen. Stephen Douglas of Illinois, was a *"noise-some, squat, and nameless animal."* He also said that South Carolina's Sen. Andrew Butler, a relative of Brooks, had taken *"a mistress – I mean, the harlot slavery."* In the honor culture of the day, a duel might have been demanded. Instead, the beating ensued inside the Capitol. Fortunately, the caning of Charles Sumner was a most rare occasion of physical violence between U.S. legislators. Yet it's common still to hear candidates tell constituents "I'll fight for you" – metaphorically. Former Vice President Al Gore once described the Presidency as *"a day-by-day fight for the people."*

Every-day politics is a battle of words rather than fists. We should expect it and adapt to it. Criticism, accusations, and investigations – though inefficient – are among the many checks against domination by any faction. It's gratifying when elected officials occasionally rise above acrimony to produce coherent, even balanced policies in areas where government is competent to do so. But governments often rule beyond their competence.

Mature people know how to take attacks and adversity in stride. It's a handy attribute in a struggling world. Social psychologist Jonathan Haidt has observed that our ability to manage adversity comes from experience. We endanger children if we shield them from early stresses and clashes:

> *Kids need conflict, insult, exclusion – they need to experience these things thousands of times when they're young in order to develop into psychologically mature adults. Every adult has to learn to handle these things and not get upset, especially by minor instances.*
>
> – Jonathan Haidt, *Misguided Minds*

Another obvious alternative to a fight is "***turning a cheek***" – a Biblical phrase for backing off, standing down, and maybe even abandoning quarrels generally. Stoics, Buddhists, and reclusive religious orders also pursue these strategies, believing that detachment can produce peace of mind. They say ambition and desire are paths to pain rather than fulfillment. Consider a Chinese Patriarch's sixth century advice:

> *If you want the truth to stand clear before you, never be for or against. The struggle between 'for' and 'against' is the mind's worst disease.*   – *Buddhist Zen master* Seng-ts'an

Being disengaged from conflict is equivalent to being a non-voter in a modern democracy. A 'disengager' invites government by someone else's preferences and priorities. Detachment breeds powerlessness and alienation. It diminishes civic connections with others. It's a high price for peace.

Another alternative to fighting is to ***divert your attention*** from conflicts, perhaps toward some form of beauty. We can withdraw particularly from

51

acts that *violate our conscience,* as did the American essayist Henry David Thoreau in 1846. Author Wendy McElroy brings vivid insight to the story:

> *Thoreau's famous act of civil disobedience was the refusal to pay a tax that supported the Mexican-American War, which he believed was immoral... As long as Thoreau was not forced to participate in this "evil" by supporting it, he seemed content to go about the business of living — of enjoying nature, family, and friends... His one night in jail came about only because the state literally knocked on his front door in the form of a tax collector. When Thoreau was released, he immediately went on a berry hunt with a swarm of young boys. No bitterness. No brooding. No lingering resentment. Without missing a beat, Thoreau simply returned to living deeply. This post-jail quest for berries occasioned my favorite line from all of Thoreau's writings: As he tramped the trails in search of juicy treasure, Thoreau found himself standing on a high point in a field. He gazed about at the continuous, sprawling beauty that surrounded him and observed "the State was nowhere to be seen."*

> *It is far more difficult today than in Thoreau's time to find places where the state cannot be seen. But, perhaps, this makes it far more important to try.* – Wendy McElroy, *The Art of Being Free*

A mountain climber offers a similar perspective on human affairs, finding diversion and perspective from eight thousand feet higher:

> *The view from the top of an eight-thousander is something you'll never forget because from up there you can actually see the Earth curving at the horizon. You really get a sense of how fragile human life is and how small it is compared to the power of nature, and you*

52

realise that the ambitions that drive us mad at sea level are completely irrelevant up there.

– Nives Meroi (mountain climber)

Studies show that experiences of awe and wonder can lower hostility, polarization, and distrust. They breed humility, connection, and openness. Consider the benefits of an *invitational* attitude, looking for opportunities to share with an adversary the experience of something beautiful, agreeable, or positive. Mood matters.

Still another choice for tangling with opponents is to ***inquire with curiosity and decency, even respect*** if possible. We might make an offer or suggestion rather than belittling or demanding; better to probe and question than to declare or seek to conquer. Rather than winning arguments, we might try instead to resolve disputes in a way that achieves much of what we want, and much of what our opponent wants as well. Said in yet other ways: **question rather than declare, explore rather than argue, listen more than tell, and reconcile if possible**.

A researcher says peace requires constructive engagement:

> *By peace we mean the capacity to transform conflicts with empathy, without violence, and creatively – a never-ending process.*

– Johan Galtung

Or Should We Avoid Arguments Altogether?

In later chapters, we'll see much more about the challenges and rewards of *seeing past our own beliefs.* Transcending our personal assumptions and boundaries helps enlarge our connections with others.

Thomas Jefferson had a strong rationale for avoiding arguments altogether. [Note: Bedlam was a nickname for London's famed Bethlem mental hospital]:

53

...never [enter] into dispute or argument with another. I never saw an instance of one of two disputants convincing the other by argument. I have seen many, on their getting warm, becoming rude, & shooting one another. ... When I hear another express an opinion which is not mine, I say to myself, he has a right to his opinion, as I to mine; why should I question it? His error does me no injury, and shall I become a Don Quixote, to bring all men by force of argument to one opinion? ... [There are] ill-tempered & rude men in society, who have taken up a passion for politics. ... Consider yourself, when with them, as among the patients of Bedlam, needing medical more than moral counsel. Be a listener only, keep within yourself, and endeavor to establish with yourself the habit of silence, especially on politics. In the fevered state of our country, no good can ever result from any attempt to set one of these fiery zealots to rights, either in fact or principle. They are determined *as to the facts they will believe, and the opinions on which they will act. Get by them, therefore, as you would by an angry bull; it is not for a man of sense to dispute the road with such an animal.* — Thomas Jefferson

Or Take It As It Comes (and Manage Attention)

Finally, when faced with a choice between peace or struggle, we may just let things unfold, and harmonize our actions with whatever occurs naturally. Making *no choice is itself a choice* – an implicit decision *not* to act. This can be an excellent option, even if we're naturally biased to action and reaction. Some problems are never solved; they are managed and outlasted. Some questions are never answered; instead they are endured.

It's said that Emperor Napoleon didn't open his mail until several weeks after it had arrived. He saved his energy for things that still required attention after the squalls had passed. This impressive deferring strategy avoids the time drain of swarming urgencies. It escapes the burden of other

54

people's sudden emergencies. It implicitly delegates less important tasks to whoever will pay attention to them; some issues and disputes are consigned to oblivion. Napoleon's method is highly relevant in our age of constant alerts, notifications, texts, tweets, posts, instant messages, Instagram stories, emails, phone calls, voicemails, texts, headlines, breaking news, and more – all competing for our attention, usually immediately.

Such constant distractions consume our mental "bandwidth" (i.e., attention). They diminish our capacity to prioritize what's important over the urgent.

Though being "connected" in cyberspace has big advantages, it also has a big price: *distraction*. Some folks find ways to completely "get off the grid" and reclaim control of their attention. It's no wonder that media companies increasingly turn to profiling technologies, and away from the clutter of interruptive advertising. It's big business to record our every online activity, monitor our physical locations as observed by cell-phone or GPS connections, organize it all as data, then sell it. Merchants pay very well for small advantages in gaining the attention of prospective buyers.

Attention has become a corollary of money: something we must pay or attract to achieve a transaction. We're deeply embedded in an attention economy. Thank you for choosing these paragraphs, right now, as something worthy of your attention!

Deciding

Decisions are mostly intuitive, based on feelings. *Sometimes* they're even supported by analysis and judgment.

Reasoning supported by columns of pros and cons (a T-chart) can eliminate bad options, but this logical method often fails to affirm a choice. Decisions are *always* about what will work best today and tomorrow, which involves uncertainty and confusion. Decisions thus turn on our confidence in what we *expect* to happen. A colleague once told me that IBM, when training him as a salesman, taught that *all buying decisions are based on emotions.* This comes down to our *confidence* about present or future usefulness. Reason is often used to justify what emotion wants. A neurologist echoes this:

Reason leads to conclusions; emotions lead to actions.   – Donald Caine

Economist Daniel Kahneman says confidence is a feeling rather than fact:

Subjective confidence in a judgment is not a reasoned evaluation of the probability that the judgment is correct. Confidence is a feeling, which reflects the coherence of the information and the cognitive ease of processing it. It is wise to take admissions of uncertainty seriously, but declarations of confidence mainly tell you that an individual has constructed a coherent story in his mind, not necessarily that the story is true.   *– Daniel Kahneman*

Confidence levels, Uncertainty, and Making Bets

We usually think of decisions as yes/no, for/against, or on/off. But dozens of daily decisions involve degrees of confidence: yes, probably, 50/50, maybe, or "probably not, but worth a shot." Sophisticated decision-makers assign big decisions a "confidence interval," stated as "X-Y% likely to succeed." Identifying a confidence interval helps manage uncertainty. It lays a foundation for later analysis to improve decision techniques.

Identifying your confidence level *at decision time* is most helpful after new information becomes available. By then we probably will have forgotten the unknowns or the errors that burdened us when the "mistake" was made.

Assigning specific confidence ratings or ranges is probably not in the cards for routine daily decisions. But thinking more carefully about confidence makes us more aware of how uncertainty, risk, confidence, and changing facts get mixed together, like a scrambled egg. Good decision-makers work over the long term to squeeze out risk for decisions that really matter.

Big decisions might benefit also from another sophisticated *prior* technique: deciding how to decide. This addresses *structure*: what factors should we consider? What information do we need? Who will be involved, using what analytical techniques? What process will be used to decide? Reaching *consensus* after hammering out differences is great; *votes* are common. In larger groups, *authorities* (especially dictators) are more efficient, but they lack the broader perspectives of a deliberative council or legislature.

A key issue here is identifying who needs to "own" (and be accountable for) a decision. A legendary story tells of Abraham Lincoln once meeting with his cabinet on a VERY important matter. After listening to their opinions and taking a vote, he announced: *"Seven nays, one aye; the ayes have it."* Though the story is probably apocryphal, it illustrates the power (and unique accountability) of the Presidency. The story symbolizes Lincoln's difficulties in managing strong opposition from advisors. This was an especially big problem in his decision to issue the Emancipation Proclamation, which his cabinet opposed.

One key aspect of decision making is a mindset of uncertainty – of awareness that little if anything is 100% right or 100% wrong. In her superb book *Thinking in Bets*, psychologist and poker professional Annie Duke notes that poker is a good metaphor for life, because *every decision we make is a bet on what will produce the best future.* Bad decisions can be obscured by a winning outcome; perfect decisions, skillfully executed and mindful of the odds, can still lose. All it takes is for that "10% chance of rain" to actually produce 100% rain in the moment. Most decisions involve some chance or luck that we must simply accept and manage, honestly and courageously. It's far better than blaming luck for our losses and taking full credit for our successes. Duke says that black and white thinking prevents us from using new information to improve ourselves:

If we think of beliefs as only 100% right or 100% wrong, when confronting new information that might contradict our belief, we have only two options: (a) make the massive shift in our opinion of ourselves from 100% right to 100% wrong, of (b) ignore or discredit the new information. It feels bad to be wrong, so we chose (b). Information that disagrees with us is an assault on our self-narrative. We'll work hard to swat that threat away.

– Annie Duke, *Thinking in Bets*

Great poker players – the ones who learn and improve – have learned to separate outcomes from quality decision rules. This avoids a sin of the gambling profession called "resulting:" a belief that winning always reflects good decisions. Great poker players are constantly re-evaluating and critically analyzing, rather than celebrating their winning brilliance or complaining about luck.

Annie Duke notes that a legendary physicist and Nobel winner showed this same thinking when he described how scientists communicate uncertainty:

Statements of science are not of what is true and what is not true, but statements of what is known to different degrees of certainty... Every one of the concepts of science is on a scale graduated somewhere between, but at neither end of, absolute falsity or absolute truth.

– Richard Feynman, *The Pleasure of Finding Things Out*

Feynman's words contain familiar themes from our earlier discussions: humility, caution, skepticism, and openness to the possibility that we can improve our imperfect beliefs.

This attitude is hard to embrace if we over-apply a pillar of western logic, called the Law of Non-Contradiction. This law says that something can't be true and false *at the same time and in the same context*. But we forget these special conditions about time and context. We remember vaguely (and falsely) that things must be either true OR false, and cannot be both. This is black/white thinking. If my belief is right, your conflicting belief must be wrong. A much better principle is that beliefs and truth propositions usually have some truth in them, but none have the whole truth. And that's exactly what we heard from psychologist Annie Duke and physicist Richard Feynman. We'll hear it later from political scientist Samuel Huntington.

Remember this always: **our beliefs are *only partly* true.** Beliefs can be improved. A "truth" can be overcome by another truth (or half-truth) that's more persuasive in a particular situation.

Procrastination and Delay

What can we say about problems that are so challenging that we can't seem to face them?

Procrastination is passive inaction. It usually suggests a lack of fortitude. Sitting for a while on a tough choice – sometimes called active waiting – can look very much like procrastination. But in truth, active waiting takes plenty of courage and restraint, biding your time for the right moment or situation to appear.

The art of timing – paying less attention to decision rules and instead emphasizing context, tradeoffs, experience, and wisdom – is worth a separate book of its own. We'll concentrate here on fatalism, the attitude of "what will be, will be." It buries our opportunities to act and change. Fatalism can look like procrastination, and both can have tragic results:

More is lost by indecision than wrong decision. Indecision is the thief of opportunity. It will steal you blind. – Marcus Tullius Cicero

Fatalism resembles stoic endurance, or "taking things as they come." Equanimity is a stable state of mind, but it lacks feeling and looks like indifference. Remember, stoicism is a strategy to avoid pain but minimizing pain is not always our main goal. Many people are superbly talented in finding ways to avoid pain or loss, which sometimes are unavoidable:

> *Hard choices involve loss — leave the marriage or stay, quit the job or take the promotion, pursue the passionate calling or choose the safe nine-to-five, move to the new city, say 'I love you.' So often, we choose not to choose, and life chooses for us, not always in our best interests.* —Janice Greenwood, writer

Failing to engage may avoid pain. More probably, it just delays it. Evading choice can disable us, as it did a U.S. presidential candidate. Thomas Dewey's listless, play-it-safe, boring campaign of 1948 ended up losing to the embattled fighter Harry Truman:

> *Dewey's chief campaign tactic was to make no mistakes, to offend no one. His major speeches, wrote the Louisville Courier Journal, could be boiled down 'to these historic four sentences: Agriculture is important. Our rivers are full of fish. You cannot have freedom without liberty. The future lies ahead.'* – David Halberstam

Instead of retreating, resigning, or evading big decisions and stubborn conflicts, sheer willpower and determined persistence are powerful long-term forces. In fact, they're two of the most powerful tools we have for making a difference. Some recovery programs urge persistence in words that also might be applied to some troubled marriages: "*Stay on the bus. The*

60

scenery will change." One American president declared that persistence (reminiscent of Angela Duckworth's Grit) is an irreplaceable force:

> *Nothing in this world can take the place of persistence. Talent will not: nothing is more common than unsuccessful men with talent. Genius will not; unrewarded genius is almost a proverb. Education will not: the world is full of educated derelicts. Persistence and determination alone are omnipotent.* – Calvin Coolidge

Deferring action and preferring delay is an observed personality style, known as "Perceiving" in the Myers-Briggs personality profile. The very name "Perceiving" indicates the benefits of this style: delay provides a chance to collect and digest more information. Perceiving is contrasted with a Judging style, which decides more quickly based on the best information available at the time. Swift judgments can reflect overconfidence or simply a bias to action. An essential rule of thumb for Judgers is to distinguish clearly between *reversible* and *irreversible* choices (though this too is a matter of degree, not a yes/no question). To restate this in more tedious language that avoids absolute thinking: *to the extent* that a choice is reversible, deciding quickly is more justified and easier, and we can change course later if necessary. *To the degree* a decision is **ir**reversible or involves high stakes, delay allows more discovery so we can act on the latest and best information.

Folk wisdom counsels us to deliberate in sayings like *haste makes waste* and *fools rush in*. Yet delay and deliberation drains time, attention, effort, and money that could be used to address other challenges. Accumulating issues grow into a carried burden – an obstacle to peace of mind. The folk saying *strike while the iron is hot* expresses the merits of deciding quickly (known as the Judging style). This advice *discourages* deliberation, as inaction can squander opportunity.

Psychologists have shown that procrastination is *not* a problem of efficiency or time management. It's about managing emotions by *evading* near-term struggle, performance anxiety, and effort. Sometimes we all avoid a hard task by indulging a pleasant distraction (such as video games, social media, a hot bath, bingeing TV, etc). We defer pain by choosing some immediate pleasure. Judgers get the pain over with and try to contain it, like ripping off a bandage, while accepting the risk that deciding sooner forecloses a later, better choice.

In deciding to strive or retreat, decide or delay, fight or submit, we know that either choice has its place and time. An ancient Jewish author beautifully expressed this poetic perspective, recounted here in part:

> *For everything there is a season, and a time for every matter under heaven:*
> *a time to be born, and a time to die; ...*
> *a time to embrace, and a time to refrain from embracing;*
> *a time to seek, and a time to lose; ...*
> *a time to keep silent, and a time to speak; ...*
> *a time for war, and a time for peace.*   *– Ecclesiastes 3:1-8 in part*

Given our many choices in engaging others, let's remember also to think carefully about the desired *outcome* and what's required to achieve it. Our desire to win may distort how we go about achieving what we really want. This point is well made in a story from ancient Greece, in Plutarch's *Lives*:

> *At the court of Pyrrhus, a Thessalonian named Cineas, a man of sound sense... had devoted himself to Pyrrhus... Seeing Pyrrhus intent upon his preparations for Italy, Cineas took an opportunity, when he saw Pyrrhus at leisure, to draw him into the following conversation: 'The Romans have the reputation of being excellent soldiers, and have the command of many warlike nations: if it please*

heaven that we conquer them, what use, Sir, shall we make of our victory?' 'Cineas,' replied the king, 'your question answers itself... When the Romans are once subdued, there is no town, whether Greek or barbarian, in all the country, that will dare oppose us; but we shall immediately be masters of all Italy... After a short pause, Cineas continued, 'But, after we have conquered Italy, what shall we do next, Sir?' Pyrrhus, not yet perceiving his drift, replied, 'There is Sicily very near... a fruitful and populous island, and easy to be taken...' 'What you say, my prince,' said Cineas, 'is very probable; but is the taking of Sicily to conclude our expeditions?' 'Far from it,' answered Pyrrhus, 'for if heaven grant us success in this, that success shall only be the prelude to greater things. Who can forbear Libya and Carthage, then within reach?... And when we have made such conquests, who can pretend to say that any of our enemies, who are now so insolent, will think of resisting us?' 'To be sure,' said Cineas, 'they will not...But when we have conquered all, what are we to do then?' 'Why, then, my friend,' said Pyrrhus, laughing, 'we will take our ease, and drink, and be merry.' Cineas, having brought him thus far replied, 'And what hinders us from drinking and taking our ease now, when we have already those things in our hands, at which we propose to arrive through seas of blood, through infinite toils and dangers, through innumerable calamities, which we must both cause and suffer?' This discourse of Cineas gave Pyrrhus pain, but produced no reformation. – Life of Pyrrhus, from Plutarch's *Lives*

King Pyrrhus strongly opposed early Rome, and was a "victor" in several battles that devastated his own forces. Pyrrhus is memorialized by the term "Pyrrhic victory," when losses are so heavy that "winning" a battle amounts to defeat. We do well to remember a Pyrrhic lesson: some victories may not be worth what we pay for them, and some cures are worse than the disease.

Conscience and Peace of Mind

According to an ancient Roman adage, there's no accounting for taste (*De gustibus non est disputandum*). We might go beyond this to say: there's no accounting for personality, character, mood, attitude, preparation, strength, and other unmeasured factors that shape our decisions on whether to struggle or settle, engage or resign, fight or flee.

Some people seem positively allergic to conflict; others despise quietness. An American playwright expressed his contempt for restful peace:

> *Better a good venereal disease than a moribund peace and quiet.*
>
> – Henry Miller

Miller appears to dread the peace of the grave. The attitude of this literary giant was shared by the "Gonzo Journalist" of the 1960s, whose words are a bit more suitable for an inspiring coffee cup inscription:

> *Life should not be a journey to the grave with the intention of arriving safely in a pretty and well-preserved body, but rather to skid in broadside in a cloud of smoke, thoroughly used up, totally worn out, and loudly proclaiming "Wow! What a Ride!"*
>
> – Hunter S. Thompson

We depart from peace every time we embrace life's ramble. Eventually we retreat again from the fray. Making mistakes, changing course, and feeling uncertain remain constant companions amid our challenges. Having a clear conscience – that is to say, a deep peace that we've done our best, and that our striving has been honest and well done – can lighten the burdens of a hectic, conflicted world. Just as forgiving others is necessary for long relationships, forgiving ourselves is key to redeeming a clear conscience from our inevitable mistakes and failures.

An eighteenth-century English genius, Samuel Johnson, elegantly asserted that *willpower* can help us relate better to others *and* to ourselves. If our emotions are not exactly warm, we can will ourselves to do gracious acts:

Kindness is in our power, even when fondness is not. –Samuel Johnson

Less articulate, but no less powerful, were the agitated words of Rodney King during the 1992 Los Angeles riots. King's street-beating by police had been captured on video and broadcast widely. When officers were acquitted from charges of using excessive violence, riots erupted. King publicly pled for calm, though not merely for his own benefit. He was anguished about the hurt descending on vulnerable, innocent others:

Can we all JUST get along? Can we get along? Can we stop making it, making it horrible for the older people and the kids?... It's just not right. It's not right. It's not, it's not going to change anything. We'll, we'll get our justice... Please, we can get along here. We all can get along. I mean, we're all stuck here for a while. Let's try to work it out. Let's try to beat it. Let's try to beat it. Let's try to work it out.

– Rodney King

Ayaan Hirsi Ali, a former Dutch politician-activist, Somali-born and now an American scholar, offers a sublimely temperate way of struggling, beginning with a look in the mirror:

Confront challenges not with outrage, but with the kind of critical thinking we Americans were once famous for, which takes self-criticism as the first step toward finding solutions. – Ayaan Hirsi Ali

Tactics for Reconciling Peace and Striving

Ponder and discuss with friends – especially those who may disagree:

1. What is worth fighting for? What's worth dying for?

2. How would you advise newlyweds to think about resolving conflicts? How would that advice differ if given to your political adversaries, to children, or to diplomats of countries on the brink of war?

3. How is respect best understood, expressed, and acted upon?

4. How do you personally manage (or balance) stability and change? Security and risk? Relationships and principles?

5. Is security found in stability and preservation, or change and adapting?

6. Assess your own patterns of stress and rest, tension and release. Are they constructive? Satisfying? Healthy?

7. Do you believe happiness is correlated with an absence of conflict?

Further Reading

Angela Duckworth	Grit
Jonathan Haidt	The Happiness Hypothesis
Stephen Pinker	Better Angels of Our Nature
Brené Brown	Dare to Lead
Paul Kalanithi	When Breath Becomes Air
Mihaly Csikszentmihalyi	Flow: A Study of Optimal Experience
David Brooks	The Second Mountain
Kirk Schneider	The Polarized Mind: Why It's Killing Us and What We Can Do About It

Now what?

A healthy balance between peace and striving straddles the healthy frontier between boredom and anxiety. At this frontier we stretch our abilities but don't overwhelm them; our tasks are not too easy, nor beyond our reach. Our appetites are satisfied. We're neither hungry nor burned out.

For healthy, growing, changing people, that frontier advances. So how high can it take us? Can some of our big dreams become reality?

Is perfection or purity an elusive ideal? Maybe we're stuck with an earthly reality that's always a bit mixed, dirty, flawed… compromised.

Our imaginations push beyond the limits of physical reality. Our ideologies operate beyond the boundaries of human nature, and but some of them seek to make human nature more perfect to meet ideological demands. How possible is that?

In the end, what can we expect of ourselves and our circumstances?

Chapter 2 – Ideals, Reality

The permanent temptation of life is to confuse dreams with reality; the permanent defeat of life comes when dreams are surrendered to reality.
  — James A. Michener

Perfectionism isn't about high standards. It's about unrealistic standards. It isn't a behavior; it's a way of thinking about yourself.
  — Andrew P. Hill, York St. John University

Don't you understand? You give up your dream, you die.
  — *Flashdance* movie

In 1825, an industrialist and social reformer named Robert Owen purchased the town of Harmony – near Evansville, Indiana – to create a utopian model of communal living and social reform. The town had been founded 11 years earlier by the Harmony Society, a communal religious group originally from Harmony, Pennsylvania (also called Rappites, for leader George Rapp). The Harmonists had moved west and south to seek lower costs, room to grow, and isolation from pesky neighbors.

Renaming the Indiana town New Harmony, Robert Owen led what would become renowned as the Owenite social experiment. Its citizens included Indiana's state geologist, who became Purdue University's first President. Another resident became a U.S. Congressman who introduced legislation to create the Smithsonian Institution in Washington. Both of these men were Robert Owen's sons. New Harmony grew to some 800 residents, became known for its research in science and education, and was selected as the second headquarters of the U.S. Geological Survey.

It was all over within two years. Owenite Josiah Warren explained that the cause of death was rivalry between individual and group interests:

It seemed that the difference of opinion, tastes and purposes increased just in proportion to the demand for conformity. Two years were worn out in this way; at the end of which, I believe that not more than three persons had the least hope of success. Most of the experimenters left in despair of all reforms, and conservatism felt itself confirmed. We had tried every conceivable form of organization and government. We had a world in miniature. – we had enacted the French revolution over again with despairing hearts instead of corpses as a result. ...It appeared that it was nature's own inherent law of diversity that had conquered us ...our 'united interests' were directly at war with the individualities of persons and circumstances and the instinct of self-preservation... and it was evident that just in proportion to the contact of persons or interests, so are concessions and compromises indispensable.

– Josiah Warren, Periodical Letter II 1856

Robert Owen's son and namesake, Robert Dale Owen – the politician and Smithsonian advocate – echoed Josiah Warren in naming a culprit. We can summarize it as the diverse, unequal talents of human beings:

[New Harmony attracted a mixed] collection of radicals, enthusiastic devotees to principle, honest latitudinarians, and lazy theorists, with a sprinkling of unprincipled sharpers thrown in...a plan which remunerates all alike, will, in the present condition of society, ultimately eliminate from a co-operative association the skilled, efficient and industrious members, leaving an ineffective and sluggish residue, in whose hands the experiment will fail, both socially and pecuniarily.

– Robert Dale Owen

70

Early America featured several other experiments to create an ideal society, including the Shakers in various locations, the Oneida Community in New York, and Brook Farm in what is now Boston:

The community of Brook Farm, Massachusetts, was founded as a community based on ideals of Transcendentalism and attracted a number of prominent intellectuals as residents and visitors. But the commune's financial state was always precarious, and Brook Farm closed in 1847. It was satirized by Nathaniel Hawthorne, who had lived there for six months, in his novel The Blithedale Romance *(1852) as a place where some residents did hours of strenuous farm work while others sat around reading poetry.*

– Encyclopedia Britannica, American Utopias

It's tempting to dream of heaven on earth. Who wouldn't want to build that? But heaven is an ideal; reality is not. We often believe in things as we want them to be, not as they are. Our illusions can be highly painful when reality asserts itself. But hope is just as essential as realism. How should we balance our dreams and common sense about what is, or what could be?

Cities or states, nations and individuals court rapid failure if their designs for the future are "unrealistic." Yet we improve and innovate based on our dreams, visions, creative ideas, and critical thinking about what "better" can look like. Technological and cultural possibility is a moving target, now more than ever. So our dreams must be agile, as expressed beautifully by a great German-American rocket scientist:

When old dreams die, new ones come to take their place. God pity a one-dream man.   – Robert Goddard

71

Is vs. Ought

What is the use of living, if it be not to strive for noble causes and to make this muddled world a better place for those who will live in it after we are gone?... How else can we put ourselves in harmonious relation with the great verities and consolations of the infinite and the eternal? And I avow my faith that we are marching towards better days. Humanity will not be cast down... We are going on swinging bravely forward along the grand high road and already behind the distant mountains is the promise of the sun.   – Winston Churchill

What a grand ideal! Better days... realized truths (verities)... consolations of the eternal... all on a sunny, grand high road beyond the mountains we climb to get there. Since 1908, when Churchill spoke those optimistic words, humanity's living standards have surged enormously. And two grisly World Wars killed or injured over 100 million people.

The bipolar realities of the 20th Century give us an occasion to ask: Should our idealism that better days are ahead ever yield to the fatalism that events could again turn violently backward? What improvements (and crises) should be expected over the next decade, and during the years after that? Most simply, what should we expect? And how can we ever reconcile the many incompatible visions of what the future could hold?

An "ideal" is a form of perfection existing only in the imagination. It's what we want to tell and believe, even if it's unlikely ever to become a reality.

We cherish ideals even more than other values, like truth. As a 20th century economist has observed:

The first thing a man will do for his ideals is lie.
    –   Joseph A. Schumpeter

Some are willing even to die for an ideal:

It is possible for a man to yield the nerve center of his consent to a purpose or cause, a movement or an ideal, which may be more important to him than whether he lives or dies.

– Howard Thurman

Those inflicting great harm may see themselves as good. A great Russian thinker saw that simple arrogance underlies the capacity for evil in everyone:

Ideology... gives the evil-doer the necessary steadfastness and determination... the social theory which helps to make his acts seem good in his own and others' eyes... In the intoxication of youthful success I had felt myself to be infallible, and I was therefore cruel.

– Aleksandr Solzhenitsyn, *The Gulag Archipelago*

An American social critic said that even laudable ideals form half of a trap:

The people in general prefer fantasy to a truthful recreation of their experience.... We are very cruelly trapped between what we would like to be and what we actually are.

– James Baldwin

The poet T.S. Eliot agreed, connecting our urge to idealize and fantasize with our wish to be right and good:

Humankind cannot bear very much reality... Half the harm that is done in this world is due to people who want to feel important. They don't mean to do harm – but the harm does not interest them. Or they do not see it, or they justify it because they are absorbed in the endless struggle to think well of themselves.

– T.S. Eliot, *The Cocktail Party*

73

Let's consider a part of reality that ancient Greeks called fate. Destiny can seem to laugh at our choices when life overruns our plans. Fate's lessons were superbly expressed by a promising young academic at Duke Divinity School, after she was stricken by a life-threatening illness:

> *Life is not a series of choices. So often the experiences that define us are the ones that we didn't pick. Cancer. Betrayal. Miscarriage. Job loss. Mental illness. A novel coronavirus.*
>
> – Kate Bowler, <u>No Cure for Being Human: And Other Truths I Need to Hear</u>

Bowler's professional research had focused – most ironically – on religious believers of the "prosperity gospel." This teaching says that God rewards his faithful followers with earthly riches and success. This message for those who fail or suffer is doubly cruel: they endure misfortune AND the clear suggestion that their suffering is deserved. Bowler's first book after her diagnosis was marvelously titled: *"Everything Happens for a Reason, And Other Lies I've Loved."*

Speaking of reason… science and rationality offer little help for identifying what *ought to be.* But scientific observation, reasoning, and critical peer review do offer powerful ways to determine *what is.* That's why science alone can't resolve political choices, which involve far more than facts:

> *Science can't determine should or shouldn't. It only informs our choices, which must ultimately be based on values and preferences.*
>
> – Theodore Zachary

We can't control many aspects of fate, but we do have some control over how we judge and respond to events. Often we don't judge very well. As the medieval political theorist Niccolò Machiavelli pointed out, most people see reality as far less compelling than *appearances.* Our sight includes mental interpretation, and it's readily distorted by what we *want* to see:

74

The great majority of mankind are satisfied with appearances, as though they were realities, and are often more influenced by the things that seem than by those that are. – Niccolò Machiavelli

As the ultimate "realist," Machiavelli said pursuing ideals can be deadly:

The gap between how people actually behave and how they ought to behave is so great that anyone who ignores everyday reality in order to live up to an ideal will soon discover that he has been taught how to destroy himself, not how to preserve himself.

– Niccolò Machiavelli

For Machiavelli, the politics of Renaissance Italy made self-preservation a street fight with little connection to moral ideals. For a prince, that daily battle was much more urgent and vital than self-improvement, self-actualization, and long-term optimal outcomes. Does that sound familiar?

The tension between high aspirations and low realities is quite ancient:

The negotiation between the utopian and the realistic, begun by Plato in The Republic, is central to political philosophy.

– Patrick Deneen, Why Liberalism Failed

Understanding and negotiating that tension, in politics but especially elsewhere, is what this chapter is about. A scholar of democracy has warned that having a realistic picture of the world and its possibilities requires us to listen broadly, sifting through many perspectives:

Listening only to one's own side can generate dangerous amounts of unrealism. – Jane Mansbridge, scholar of democratic theory

***

Perfection and Purity

Utopias are fantasies. Both are commonly found in entertainment and literature. Utopian fiction explores what Wikipedia calls the "attributes of another reality that is intended to appeal to readers." It's probably more accurate to say that utopian fiction explores the attributes of *an author's* fantasy, because imaginative "other realities" rarely exist in a material way. The fantasy category also includes dystopian fiction and horror movies, which envision realities we fear and loathe. Virtual reality, for good or bad, is a rapidly expanding category that will reshape the characteristics and boundaries of what we consider to be "real," both good and bad.

Remarkably, many constructive fantasies of the past have become real:

- Air travel was long an imagined fantasy, until it became a reality in 1903. Space travel was impossible until the 1950s. Landing a spacecraft on the moon was fantasy until Russia did it in 1959; landing humans there took the U.S. another decade, until 1969. America's unmanned mission to another planet (Mars) landed in 1976. Travel to stars and galaxies are still dreams, far beyond our available technology – but they're considered hypothetically possible.
- Jules Verne's 1869 story, *20,000 Leagues Under the Seas,* imagined the future of submarine travel, which expanded impressively in the 20th century. It's now routine for military purposes.
- Many other things we now take for granted appeared earlier in the imagination of a science fiction writer:

- Credit cards	- communication satellites	- military tanks
- driverless cars	- email	- anti-depressants
- electric cars	- earbuds	- waterbeds
- elevators	- real-time translation	- Big Brother
- video calls	- 3D printers	surveillance

According to the father of the U.S. space program, dreams have a way of becoming hopes, and then realities:

> *It is difficult to say what is impossible; for the dream of yesterday is the hope of today and the reality of tomorrow.*
>
>   – Robert H. Goddard

A popular science fiction writer powerfully expresses the attraction of science fiction, which probes beyond today's frontier of possibility:

> *The limits of the possible can only be defined by going beyond them into the impossible.*   – Arthur C. Clarke

This is known as Clarke's Second Law. Clarke also formulated a Third Law that describes how "advanced" technologies fascinate us like magic:

> *Any sufficiently advanced technology is indistinguishable from magic.*
>
>   – Arthur C. Clarke

Clarke's *First* Law is also illuminating. It declares that science can confirm what we know to be possible, but it cannot reliably declare what is impossible:

> *When a distinguished but elderly scientist states that something is possible, he is almost certainly right. When he states that something is impossible, he is very probably wrong.*
>
>   – Arthur C. Clarke

If you'd like to be terrifically entertained by how experts can be so wrong about the possible future, find a copy of *The Experts Speak,* by Cerf and Navasky. Here's a glimpse:

The brain is an organ of minor importance.
− Aristotle

There is not the slightest indication that [nuclear]energy will ever be obtainable. − Albert Einstein

We don't like their sound. Groups of guitars are on the way out.
− Decca Recording Co. exec, turning down the Beatles, 1962

There is no reason for any individual to have a computer in their home.
− President of Digital Equipment Corporation, 1977

We're having some fun at the expense of "experts," but we do no better. Try describing the world of 10-20 years from now; seal it to be read then. It will be good for a future laugh! We needn't be ashamed of our blindness about the future; any scenario is necessarily imaginary. None of it yet real. Reason and logic can project trends, but not creativity and innovation − which happen to depend heavily on imagination.

Diplomacy is an area where realism and ideology may severely conflict. According to Henry Kissinger, realists (like himself, a.k.a. "power people") are those who probe what's possible according to the facts on the ground. In contrast, idealists (who he calls "prophets") work toward a high-minded vision of what *should be*. Idealists have moral, ethical, and political concerns ranging from human rights to democratic norms. These concerns sit uneasily in some cultures − especially those who are highly group-oriented, or under heavy central authority. Idealists demand policy principles acceptable to *us* on religion, climate, trade policy, regulation, and other ethically sensitive areas:

78

The idealists are presumed to be the noble people, and the power people are the ones who [supposedly] cause all the world's trouble. But I believe more suffering has been caused by prophets than statesmen... The art of good foreign policy is to understand and to take into consideration the values of a society, to realize them at the outer limit of the possible.

– Henry Kissinger, quoted by Jeffrey
Fields, *Lessons in Realpolitik*

If we're tempted to think we can achieve perfection in an imperfect world, we're in for a lot of disappointment and forgiveness. Yet a desire for "perfection" as a kind of guiding star certainly can motivate and discipline us to get ever closer to our ideals.

Discussing our desire for perfection brings to mind a cherished story featuring West Tennessee humor. Cousin Glen once said that he'd received some farm vegetables from a friend, who later asked how he liked them. This friend was close enough that Glen could reply:

They were perfect! If those veggies had been any better you wouldn't have given them to me, and if they'd been any worse I couldn't have eaten 'em. – Glen M.

Sounds to me like the realist Henry Kissinger!

***

The word utopia, from Latin for 'no place' or 'good place,' gives further clues that utopias are imaginary rather than achievable. The word was first used when Sir Thomas More imagined a perfect society in *Utopia* (1516). Plato's *Republic* (~375 BC) describes the political system of an ideal society (but to most modern eyes, Plato's vision was seriously flawed).

John Winthrop, a Puritan leader in the earliest American settlements, preached in 1630 that *"we shall be as a City upon a Hill, the eyes of all people are upon us."* Winthrop was describing the Puritan mission – an idealistic wish – to create in America an example of a caring, loving, selfless, purer community. This was unlike the reality Puritans were fleeing. It also was quite unlike the Puritanical society they created.

In 1961 U.S. President-elect John Kennedy used Winthrop's "City on a Hill" imagery to describe his mission as President: to create a better society. On election eve in 1980, Ronald Reagan joined the tradition and added a word ("a *shining* city on a hill"). Critics saw this as a statement of American exceptionalism; others admired Reagan's patriotic idealism.

Regardless of how all of these declarations may be interpreted, all are easily seen as *ideals*. To whatever degree any of our ideals approach perfection, they never become reality. There's no single, unifying concept of perfection that we could actualize; there's no single "right way." Remember that this book is about the ferocious conflicts between diverse (yet separately valid) values. People are never even close to perfect, so our diversity sits uneasily with the more singular idea of "perfection." America's founding fathers had human imperfection squarely in mind as they designed a new system of government:

> *But what is government itself, but the greatest of all reflections on human nature? If men were angels, no government would be necessary. If angels were to govern men, neither external nor internal controls on government would be necessary.*
>
> – James Madison, Federalist No. 51

For centuries, the "American Dream" has been a reality for waves of U.S. immigrants, envisioning better times. This "dream" clearly is a goal or a vision, seeing a future with fewer shortcomings and more opportunities.

It's a way of thinking about what *can be*, and what one day *may be*. Unfortunately, every reality turns out to be far from perfect. We occasionally experience a fantastic inspiration or exalted mood, which can make things seems perfect for a while. But alas, bliss is fleeting.

If we're wise, we use dreams for motivation, then tackle the hard task of achieving what's really possible. Yet as we've seen in prior pages from 'leading experts,' being confident about what's possible is a dubious proposition at best, especially if it involves people. So we must estimate and optimize, using our always-limited knowledge.

Scholar Thomas Sowell sees that some people accept, and others deny, the existence of natural and permanent limits for what's possible. He describes a *constrained vision* that says human and natural shortcomings require choices between imperfect alternatives. An *unconstrained vision* claims that knowledge, people, and societies are continually "perfectible":

> *The notion that "the human being is highly plastic material" is still central among many... who share the unconstrained vision... Man is, in short, perfectible – meaning continually improvable rather than capable of reaching absolute perfection... [and] efforts must be made to wake the sleeping virtues of mankind... Condorcet anticipated the eventual "reconciliation, the identification, of the interests of each with the interests of all" – at which point "the path of virtue is no longer arduous"... William Godwin and Condorcet did not rule out an eventual conquest of death... Intentions, which were crucial in the unconstrained vision of Godwin, were irrelevant in the constrained vision of Adam Smith... The moral limitations of man in general, and his egocentricity in particular, were neither lamented by Smith nor regarded as things to be changed. They were treated as inherent facts of life... The fundamental moral and social challenge was to make the best of*

the possibilities... rather than dissipate energies in an attempt to change human nature – an attempt that Smith treated as both vain and pointless... One of the hallmarks of the constrained vision is that it deals in trade-offs rather than solutions...While believers in the unconstrained vision seek the special causes of war, poverty, and crime, believers in the constrained vision seek the special causes of peace, wealth, and a law-abiding society.

– Thomas Sowell, *A Conflict of Visions*

Sowell's fantastic book says these competing visions don't line up strictly with political loyalties, though "*the unconstrained vision is more at home on the political left.*" Political scientist Charles Murray denies this idea that socio-political policies can transform human nature at a large scale:

One of the Left's most crippling errors for a century now has been to discount the importance of innate and intractable human nature, insisting instead that human tendencies are malleable and that the behavior of large numbers of humans can be changed by design given the right social policies.   – Charles Murray

A better alignment than left/right may be to say that an unconstrained view strongly aligns with idealism. The book you're reading aligns squarely with the constrained vision that perfection is not remotely possible – that we can't 'have it all.' This view means we're forced to trade-off one good with another, never fully having both. Important historical figures have aligned with either of these visions in unpredictable ways. Sowell says that unconstrained thinkers include Voltaire, Thomas Paine, Jean-Jacques Rousseau, George Bernard Shaw, Robert Owen (of New Harmony fame), and Supreme Court Justice Earl Warren. Constrained thinkers include the authors of The Federalist Papers, Adam Smith, Thomas Hobbes, Edmund Burke, Supreme Court Justice Oliver Wendell Holmes, Milton Friedman, and Friedrich Hayek.

Václav Havel – a Czechoslovakian playwright, dissident, and President after the Czech revolt against communism – was unsatisfied with his country's view of 'what's possible.' Though an anti-communist, he leaned in at least some ways toward Sowell's unconstrained category. Havel's 1997 book of collected lectures was entitled *The Art of the Impossible*, an artful phrase showing his ambition to do "impossible" things. Havel knows there *are* limits to what's possible, but he wants to push beyond the low expectations of others, starting with their consciousness:

> *The salvation of this human world lies nowhere else than in the human heart, in the human power to reflect, in human modesty, and in human responsibility. Without a global revolution in the sphere of human consciousness, nothing will change for the better."*
> – Václav Havel, *The Art of the Impossible: Politics as Morality in Practice*

Havel modeled his title to transcend the words of a 19th century German Chancellor, whose constrained vision had dominated much of Europe:

> *Politics is the art of the possible, the attainable – the art of the next best.*
> – Otto von Bismarck

Long before Havel, Hillary Clinton also riffed on Bismarck's words while echoing Robert Kennedy as well ("*I dream of things that never were and ask why not?*"). Clinton's remarks about this were in her well-known student speech in a 1969 graduation ceremony from Wellesley College:

> *We feel that for too long our leaders have viewed politics as the art of the possible. And the challenge now is to practice politics as the art of making what appears to be impossible possible.*
> – Hillary Clinton

Pushing to exceed limits is a common task for athletes, who train heavily to improve their "personal best" and break records. Pushing boundaries is a key task in military boot camps, which attack the mental limits that can reduce physical endurance and presence of mind during combat. A whole industry of motivational specialists teaches that we can do more than we ever imagined. They're probably right, though most self-help doesn't produce our lasting best selves, but rather a pale imitation that nudges us upward, slightly, until stubborn old habits usually return. A lot of wasted human potential is out there, even as we try again and again to harness it.

Life's burdens are temporarily lifted when we indulge flights of fancy. Many books and movies do precisely this. Fiction at its best lets our imaginations roam; it diverts attention from troubles and expands our view of what could be. We're more free in a spirited, unreal kind of way:

The ultimate freedom is substituting fantasy for reality.
— Encyclopedia Of World Problems

It's worth noting that illusions help us visualize hopes, relieve despair, and boost self-esteem. We tell ourselves that we're basically in control (whether true or not)... that we can escape troubles for a problem-free life (not likely)... and that we're better than we actually are. We indulge ideals and wishes in our imaginations. Then we try to realize them more fully in daily reality.

Escape into fantasy can be constructive, relieving, and hopeful if we firmly understand that fantasies are *not materially real or true*. A cultivated imagination is powerful for good or ill, but we mustn't let it deceive us about what to expect outside the imagination. In a way, imagination is like money – a good servant and a poor master.

Unicorns, fairies, mermaids and elves appear to be harmless fantasies for children. But they serve a constructive purpose: developing what psychologists call "counterfactual reasoning." In simpler words, imagination improves our ability to understand *what would happen if things were different.* This skill, developed in playful pretending, has obvious adult application to innovation (in technology, industry, etc.) and to creative people at any age. We might even think of "counterfactual reasoning" as creativity or innovation throughout life. For example, a supercomputer inventor has said he dealt with conceptual stumbling blocks by physically digging in the dirt under his home:

> *While I'm digging in the tunnel the elves will often come to me with solutions to my problem.* — Seymour Crey

More potent children's fantasies include Santa Claus and Prince Charming. Ancient Greek mythology told of satyrs and fauns (half-human and half-animal) as well as Dionysus (half-man and half-god). Little birdies, talking snakes and dragons symbolize secretive allies and powerful enemies. Most potent of all, we symbolize good and evil in our speculations about angels or devils, heaven or hell.

Whatever may be the merits of fantasy, it's tragic if we surrender our fantastical dreams of becoming better, feeling better, doing better. It's also tragic to lose our sense of realistic proportion and control over threats and dangers. As we saw at the very beginning of this chapter:

> *The permanent temptation of life is to confuse dreams with reality; the permanent defeat of life comes when dreams are surrendered to reality.* — James A. Michener

What's possible within human limits? Our maximum lifespan is said to be 120-130 years, but we really don't know what it could be, do we?

Imagination on this topic is alive and well. Some think that in future centuries we may live 1000+ years (according to Aubrey de Grey), or eliminate death entirely (so say Joon Yun and Martine Rothblatt). Futurist Ray Kurzweil predicts that human and artificial intelligence will synthesize into new life forms. These visions are certainly not yet true, and we simply don't know whether they could become so.

What's the perfect human life? We don't know that, either – except to say with confidence (never certainty!) that nobody will ever have one.

How pure can we be? Like perfection, absolute purity is an ideal. Pure conviction (untainted by doubt) is a mighty force, but demands for pure social groups tends to put one in a minority. More purity = more minority. The purest faction has a membership of one. And even a single person may have several inconsistent opinions about complicated topics.

The actor Leonard Nimoy, a few days before he died, observed that a sense of perfection can be sustained in memory:

> *A life is like a garden. Perfect moments can be had but only*
> *preserved in memory.*   – Leonard Nimoy

We live each day in an imperfect, impure reality – and are the richer for it.

> *Things are never perfect, but they can be just right.*
>   – Little Women 2018 PBS production

***

Imperfection and Failure

The study of history is a powerful antidote to contemporary arrogance. It is humbling to discover how many of our glib assumptions, which seem to us novel and plausible, have been tested before, not once but many times and in innumerable guises; and discovered to be, at great human cost, wholly false.

– Paul Johnson, *The Quotable Paul Johnson*

Teenagers and young adults typically are on fire about changing the world. They see injustices, mistakes, so many faults – and are determined to fix them. Or at least they want to make the world better. We need their energy and ambition. Generations of such people have made the world a better place – better now, in so many ways, than ever before.

Yet these teenagers and young adults also have blind spots (like all of us), and they lack the wisdom of experience. They seem unaware that some of their most urgent ideas have been tried before and failed miserably. After Marxist ideology in the 20th century led to death for tens (if not hundreds) of millions of people – notably in China, Russia, and eastern Europe – some still insist that real Marxism hasn't been tried. They believe it should be. Millions more may be killed before inexperienced ideologues, and others who refuse to learn, have absorbed a lesson that's so apparent to others. One brilliant philosopher puts the matter succinctly:

Those who cannot remember the past are condemned to repeat it.

– George Santayana

Another top-shelf thinker, Karl Popper, observed that "*Those who promise us paradise on earth never produced anything but a hell.*" This forcefully restates the proverb that "*the road to hell is paved with good intentions.*"

Repeated historical failures are supported usually by confident words, including *"this time it's different."* Occasionally the words are right, as with Thomas Edison's legendary 10,000[th] try to invent the light bulb. But more commonly, exceptional behaviors and events *revert to the mean.* They return to a norm, just as a pendulum does. This statistical principle says that high and low, good and bad usually return to a more normal balance, or equilibrium. Accurate expectations incorporate that fact.

Our world is indeed broken in many ways. Ancient Hebrew scriptures, in their creation stories, describe the very beginning of the world as a fall from grace, a corruption with permanent consequences for the human condition. Nobody was actually present to report what happened at 'the beginning.' But the Bible's creation mythology presents a powerful moral view that humans are flawed, limited, and incapable of becoming perfect.

If ever we're tempted to overlook our flaws (i.e., almost every day), we can count on being reminded of them by opposing partisans. Politicians tread a fine line between criticizing, accusing, and blaming as they suggest potential improvements and maneuver to achieve them:

> *[Some] politicians are always rubbing your face in some national moral deficiency or failure.*   – Daniel Henninger

Our imperfection isn't just moral. Evolution adapts and refines creatures over time, but in so doing it sometimes produces physical compromises that are far from optimal or functional:

> *[Humans have] useless earlobes, their tedious wisdom teeth... their vermiform intestinal appendage [the appendix], their spinal curves, and their vas deferens, which carries sperm from the testicles to the penis not directly and by the shortest route but instead after going by a useless and lengthy route via the ureter...*

[they have] the remains of their ancestral quadrupedal gait, and the corresponding ills and pains [of walking upright:] backache, sciatica, flat feet, scoliosis, and hernias... Evolution is not perfect but is rather the result of unstable and precarious compromises.

– Telmo Pievani, *Imperfection: A Natural History*

A reviewer of Pievani's book piles on even more defects in nature's most refined creatures, the humans at the 'top of the food chain:'

Add the terrible structure of our knees, our lower backs, the fact that the opening of the tubes carrying food and air are so close that choking is a significant cause of mortality, the awkwardness of having our reproduction and sewerage emerging right next to each other. We are shot through with deficiencies that wouldn't earn even a passing grade for a novice bioengineer, never mind an omniscient, omnipotent deity... fundamentalists on both extremes of the evolution divide misinterpret perfection: creationists proclaim that only a supreme being could have produced such superb complexity, while hyper-adaptationists emphasize the power of natural selection to achieve the same thing, promoting a "gee whiz" perspective on evolution.

– David P. Barash, psychology professor emeritus

So in the end, how best do we improve our diminished state of being? Make money? A multi-billionaire answers clearly:

Anybody who thinks money will make you happy hasn't got money.
– David Geffen

A scholar who studies our use of time and its impact on happiness describes what money can and can't do:

The best data suggests money protects against sadness, but doesn't buy joy... When our car breaks down, money provides a solution to this very specific stressor. True happiness requires an investment of our attention and our time.

— Ashley Whillans, Harvard Business School

How about ambition, then? A top Hollywood actor, having reached the pinnacle of stardom, warns us not to raise our hopes that achievement will make us whole:

When you get to the top, just remember there's nothing there. The only thing that really matters is love. No matter what your accomplishments are, it's incredible lonely if you're not surrounded by some form of love.

—Nicole Kidman, actor

A great American novel, *The Great Gatsby*, portrays a common American delusion that dreams, willpower, hope, sheer wits, and gumption can deliver us the promised land of love and prosperity:

In Jay Gatsby, [F. Scott] Fitzgerald gave us our most radiant example of a romantic New World type: the self-deluded true believer. Every American likes to think he can make himself anew and dream himself into a happier future, just as James Gatz did by changing his name, burying his past, living by his wits and winning his fortune, all while longing for something still more – his elusive old flame, Daisy Buchanan.   *— Lauren Weiner, writer*

A young surgeon, fully aware that cancer soon would end his life, offered his perspective on failure, struggle, and the effort to transcend them:

The secret is to know that the deck is stacked, that you will lose, that your hands or judgment will slip, and yet still struggle to win... You can't ever reach perfection, but you can believe in an asymptote toward which you are ceaselessly striving.

– Paul Kalanithi, *When Breath Becomes Air*

Japanese "wabi sabi" is the beauty of *im*perfection. Their art form called Kintsugi actually celebrates brokenness by repairing cracks and chips with gold. Imperfect objects in Japan, exhibiting what Shakespeare called 'the slings and arrows of outrageous fortune,' can be more valuable than perfect ones. Think of the meaning and value attached to artifacts from the Titanic, or the wreckage of New York's World Trade Center. Practitioners of Kintsugi cherish fractures:

[Kintsugi is] the art of mending cracks without secret. Of repairing while exposing the point of fracture... Something that has survived damage can be considered more valuable, more beautiful.

– Andres Neuman, author of 'Fracture'

As for people, we mend cracks in ourselves, but mending cracks in other people is another matter altogether:

I have learned not to correct people even when I know they are wrong. The onus of making everyone perfect is not on me. Peace is more precious than perfection.

– https://spiritdaily.org/blog/news/what-i-learned-after-i-reached-70

Kindness is a good first step toward improvement. Good follow-ons include generosity and acceptance. Maybe even love will flower, as envisioned by 1960s calls for "Peace and Love." Universal love is an idyllic dream, a worthy ideal... but anyone who thinks they can love everybody simply hasn't met enough people.

Humans fail to measure up in so many ways. We're known for vices like greed, pride, and envy, yet we still can be filled with joy, creativity, achievement, and laughter. We can cherish our scars; they're monuments to living in an imperfect world. In this reality, finding satisfaction and peace requires letting go of the conceit that we're nearly perfect, having few vices that matter. It requires being comfortable with forgiveness and acceptance, which are the foundations of wholeness and reconciliation.

And now that you don't have to be perfect, you can be good.
— John Steinbeck

Imagination

Imagination is more important than knowledge. For knowledge is limited, whereas imagination embraces the entire world, stimulating progress, giving birth to evolution. — Albert Einstein

In his masterful 2004 book *The Curse of the Self*, Prof. of Psychology and Neuroscience Mark Leary says self-awareness is a blessing and a curse. On the plus side, it empowers us to think of ourselves abstractly in time; a sense of time allows us to reinterpret the past and reimagine the future. Abstract thinking helps us develop moral concerns about other souls, rather than seeing them as objects or beings to overcome. But self-awareness is also a curse: memories can bring regrets, and ongoing awareness of the uncertain future leads us to worry.

On this telling, self-awareness and its relatives – abstract thinking, imagination, a concept of time – are at the core of who we are as humans. These powerful characteristics put humans at the top of the food chain, so to speak. We're not yet quite as resilient as cockroaches (200,000 years for us, 200+ million years for them), but I wouldn't trade places.

So, what are the consequences of these nearly unique human abilities? First, we usually think very highly of ourselves:

> *Everyone is necessarily the hero of his own imagination.*
>
> – John Barth, author

> *As humans we have an unstoppable impulse to valorize our own memories.* – Malcolm Gladwell, author

We also have an enormous capacity for self-determination:

> *If one advances confidently in the direction of his dreams, and endeavors to live the life which he has imagined, he will meet with a success unexpected in common hours.*
>
> – H.D. Thoreau, essayist

We envision things and make them happen:

> *This wall will fall. Beliefs become reality.*
>
> – graffiti artist, Berlin Wall

> *You take a dream, and you build a dream, and you keep building on it and you don't let anybody stop you.* – Chuck Peddle, engineer

> *If you don't follow your dream, then you will work for someone who did.*
>
> – promotion for franchise businesses

Imagination fills a void, and we create stories to deal with frightening unknowns.

> *Humans are pattern-seeking story-telling animals, and we are quite adept at telling stories about patterns, whether they exist or not.*
>
> – Michael Shermer, author, *Why People Believe Weird Things*

Failure to explain a threat leads to anxiety and fear, so our minds fill the gap with imagined explanations. We also do this unconsciously: when sensory information is missing, our brains will infer what's needed to conclude that we've seen or heard a sensible pattern. Optical illusions are precisely about filling in missing information: our vision switches between two possible ways of interpreting an incomplete, ambiguous image. The brain also does strange things when the eyes send jumbled signals, so that people with failing vision may hallucinate.

Our powers of reason can operate the same way, by creating a story. Think of how we explain a sudden death: we're being punished, or it's God's will... *anything* that establishes an understandable cause. With a plausible cause in mind, maybe we can prevent another tragedy tomorrow. In the Hebrew Bible, ancient Jews repeatedly blame their own lack of faith as a cause of their defeats and disasters. At least they might influence future tragedies if only they'd be more faithful. One theologian expresses her feelings after learning her child had an untreatable illness:

> *The helplessness was unacceptable... I realized that I was making myself feel guilty, and that I would rather feel guilty than helpless.*
>
> – Elaine Pagels

Beliefs provide explanations and consolation amid great unknowns. They make life sensible and bearable. It's little wonder that we defend our beliefs with such fierceness, and conflicting views cause such problems.

Religion draws heavily on imagination to deal with questions that cannot go unanswered, dismissed with a shrug of the shoulders. Why did my child have to die? Where did we come from, and what causes creation? Where are we going? Is "spirit" something beyond individual consciousness and brain processes? What is love?

Reason and science now provide ever more clues to such questions. But for most of history they offered little or nothing. Even after five centuries of empirical science, so much remains unobserved and unknown.

Religious sensibilities draw on the imagination with imagery and poetry – and most of all with symbols. Religion's elusive truths, though very real to believers, aren't directly observable; they're represented and expressed with symbols. In *A Journey Through The Hebrew Scriptures*, Prof. Frank Frick identifies over three dozen types of literature in the Bible. Some are prose (stories, sermons, biography, discourse, admonition, history, etc.). But many types of scriptural literature are more symbolic, especially parables, riddles, and allegories among those few listed here:

allegory	fable	poetry
aphorism	legend/saga	parable
apocalyptic	oracle	riddle

Images have been historically important, especially for communicating with illiterate people via signs, stained glass windows, trademarks, and more. Even now, with widespread literacy in our visually intensive modern cultures, symbols powerfully indicate connections, commitments, and beliefs. Especially for religious people, symbols are gateways to essential truth:

Everything is a symbol if you're seeking the truth. – Jacob Needleman

Sigmund Freud was a big believer in psychological symbolism for subconscious urges, especially sexual ones. But he denied that *everything* is a symbol:

Sometimes a cigar is just a cigar.   – Sigmund Freud

***

There is a heavy role for imagination in poetry, art, and music. Even science requires imagination to create theories that explain facts. Minds create the building blocks of civilizations. Humans create conscious communities at an enormously larger scale than any other beings. Cyberspace, augmented reality (AR) and virtual reality (VR) are just the latest imaginative additions to our human experience. But they're not "reality" any more than TV or movies are. AR and VR extend far beyond the physical world, which has always *embodied* intangible, metaphysical things like spirits, minds, emotions, visions, and imaginations. Cyberspace, AR, and VR are not physically real; they are *disembodied* and metaphysical, for good or ill.

Just as the car we drive can seem to mentally extend our bodies, in time people will adapt to more recently new metaphysical realms. Our imaginations will become interwoven with VR, AR, and cyberspace – as they already are with television, movies, plays, and video games:

George Gerbner's "cultivation theory" hypothesizes that the more television people watch, the more they begin to believe that television mirrors reality instead of being stylized for dramatic effect.

– Rebecca Renner, National Geographic magazine

Some artists value their imaginative world more than their material reality:

As an artist since I can remember, I always felt that the "real" world was not the phenomenal world I was living in and negotiating each day. I strongly intuitively felt and believed (and still do) that the real world is my own imagination and the art is a consequence of that. The challenge is to remain in that place as much as possible as the world wants to claim its piece!   – Joseph Sulkowski, painter

Joseph also attests that being artful also requires the artist to leave something to the observer's imagination.

"Lovely intangibles" is a lovely way to describe the benefits of an artful or spiritual imagination. One author's praise for ethereal things comes with strongly negative attitude about materialistic points of view:

Some of the greatest intangibles are Love, Hope, and Wonder. Another is Deity. Is it folly to believe in something that is intangible? The choice to be a fool is yours.

> – Vera Nazarian, *The Perpetual Calendar of Inspiration*

Consider our sense of elevation on certain days of the year: Valentine's Day inspires sweethearts, July 4th stirs American patriots, and Easter is special for Christians. At Christmas even many non-Christians join the appreciation for kinship, innocence and joy in children, and the powerful pull of home.

Oh, Christmas isn't just a day, it is a frame of mind.

> – Kris Kringle, *Miracle on 34th Street*

A child's reality involves a great deal of imagination, and the boundaries between fact and fantasy can be dim. Some adults draw very bright lines, insisting that the "lovely intangibles" (such as souls, spirits, and deities) are magical, superstitious beliefs based in ignorance of physical laws. From a strictly materialist point of view, such strict boundaries can be very useful – yet much depends on how we reconcile physical and ephemeral, body and spirit, rational and irrational. That's a skill of maturity. At some age we must expose children to a more grounded understanding of reality. Pop star Stevie Wonder declares that superstitions – magical ideas about things we don't understand – are an open invitation for suffering:

When you believe in things / That you don't understand / Then you suffer / Superstition ain't the way. Very superstitious, nothin' more to say / Very superstitious, the devil's on his way.

> – Stevie Wonder, *Superstition*

Nearly two millennia ago an Egyptian astronomer, mathematician, and philosopher demanded that superstitions must *not* be taught as truth:

Fables should be taught as fables, myths as myths, and miracles as poetic fancies. To teach superstitions as truths is a most terrible thing. The child mind accepts and believes them, and only through great pain and perhaps tragedy can he be in later years relieved of them. In fact, men will fight for a superstition quite as quickly as for a living truth — often more so, since a superstition is so intangible you cannot get at it to refute it, but truth is a point of view, and so is changeable.   – Hypatia of Alexandria

Despite the demands of reason, facts, common sense, and materialism, the "lovely intangibles" of imagination are among the things we most cherish: trust, kindness, joy, affection, and love. Imagination is where belief has its most powerful hold on us. Observation and science can't operate there.

Simply believing in something (like love, or kindness, or generosity) can make it appear more frequently in our lived experience. We see what we believe, and act accordingly. For others, opposite beliefs (e.g., that exploitation prevails) also can be self-fulfilling. The knee-jerk reactions of motivated reasoning operate across the spectrum of belief.

Martin Seligman, the creator of Positive Psychology (the scientific study of life's positive events and influences) affirms that attitudes can bias outcomes in what seems to be very nearly a case of "mind over matter":

[According to Martin Seligman], by thinking optimistically, you can change things for the better. Conversely, by thinking pessimistically, you can change things for the worse.   – Diana Rabb, author and speaker

We suffer incalculable losses if our lives become failures of imagination.

Reality

Before discussing this 'non-fantastic' topic, let's be sure we're on the same page about what reality actually is. The next page or two may strike some readers as delicately nuanced, or overly nuanced — but stick with me for a vitally important clarification about perceptions and reality.

Many define reality as *objective facts*. They exist whether or not we see them:

> *Reality is that which, when you stop believing in it, doesn't go away.*
> — Philip K. Dick, *I Hope I Shall Arrive Soon*

We perceive this objective reality either accurately or inaccurately. But a rival understanding of reality says that our minds actively filter through sensory information, seeing primarily *what we expect and want* to see:

> *For millennia, philosophers have understood that we don't see life as it is; we see a version distorted by our hopes, fears, and other attachments.* – Lukianoff & Haidt, *The Atlantic*

We hear something other than what's said or intended. Our senses differ as well. Some delight in the aroma of fresh cilantro; for others a gene makes it taste like soap. Most can close their eyes and see imaginary images, but the 1-3% with aphantasia cannot; they often don't know that a "mind's eye" is possible. Color blindness and light sensitivity, deafness or noise sensitivity, unusual tolerances for heat or cold, damaged nerves, attention disorders, psychiatric conditions, boredom or overstimulation, and countless other factors shape our sensory inputs even before our brains interpret them.

As others have said: *We see things not as they are, but as we are* – we see what we're *able* to perceive, or *conditioned* to perceive, or *want* to perceive. A neuroscientist says that even the simple act of walking into a room engages our brain in a particularly self-centered way:

What you experience are the brain's deductions about the relevance of objects or a room's layout to you, to your survival, and to your goals. – Patrick House

Because of our mental filters and expectations, seeing is not believing; *believing is seeing.* Yet another version of this distorting effect came from a Harvard instructor in 1891 (when all his students were men):

Every man looks through the eyes of his prejudices, of his preconceived notions. Hence, it is the most difficult thing in the world to broaden a man so that he will realize truth as other men see it.
– Samuel Silas Curry, *The Province of Expression*

Ah, we're back to the truth that doesn't go away if nobody sees or believes it. That "truth as [others also] see it" refers to *objective reality*. It's the kind of truth that scientists look for, viewable by any fair observer. Objective truth requires fair observers to agree they've seen the same thing. The techniques of science rub away specific points of view. They make an end run around subjective screens and distortions, like beliefs and wishes.

But *subjective* reality is what we experience every day, shaped by our experiences, memories, beliefs, expectations, prejudices, and biases. For each person, subjective perceptions construct *my truth* – and others don't see the same thing. Subjectivism leads each of us to experience a reality that's different from that of any other person.

Most of us, most of the time, live with the unquestioned belief that the world looks as it does because that's the way it is. There is one small step from this belief to another: "Other people view the world much the way I do." These beliefs, which have been called naïve realism, are essential to a sense of reality we share with other people. We rarely question those beliefs. We hold a single interpretation of the

100

world around us at any one time, and we normally invest little effort in generating plausible alternatives to it. One interpretation is enough, and we experience it as true. We do not go through life imagining alternative ways of seeing what we see.

– Kahneman, Sibony, & Sunstein: Noise

So everyone's subjective reality differs from every other person's – marginally or maybe enormously.

Each of us thinks we see objective reality, but we don't. Nobody's personal reality matches objective reality. For this reason, eyewitness testimony is considered a weak form of evidence. Even if people insist "*I saw it with my own eyes*," their brain has *interpreted* what their limited eyes captured. As we'll discuss elsewhere, all this has profound consequences for what we consider to be knowledge… how we fight over what's "right" or "fake"… and how we struggle so mightily to understand and relate to each other.

It gets more complicated. For Kate Bowler, a life-threatening diagnosis made her realize that she had been living not so much in her *present* reality. She had been living in her imagined future, now radically changed:

If I were to invent a sin to describe… how I lived… It was the sin of arrogance, of becoming impervious to life itself. I failed to love what was present and decided to love what was possible instead.

– Kate Bowler, <u>Everything Happens for a Reason: And Other Lies I've Loved</u>

Objective or subjective, present or past, or imagined realities – each is simply one of many versions of truth and experience. In any moment we have the power to choose between them. It's challenging enough to try grasping all those realities for just one person. Add to this all such realties for just one other person (not to mention close friends, acquaintances, adversaries in public controversies, pundits, politicians, etc.) and we're lost in high cotton.

For me, potential answers to this problem are:

- humility and openness, grasping for more insight into the things we all experience or imagine in common
- persistent awareness that appearances aren't truth, and my perceptions often mislead me
- steady effort to see things more as they are, and as others see them – not so much *as I wish them to be*

An Italian physicist has described well the latest understandings in quantum mechanics and what they say about physical reality. Though quantum laws are weird and quirky, they repeatedly have been proven to be true and useful, notably in advanced technologies. High-tech science suggests to us some fresh ways to think about our own realities.

> *The equations of quantum mechanics are used daily... They are extremely useful in all contemporary technology... but they remain mysterious. Quantum mechanics and experiments with particles have taught us that the world is a continuous, restless swarming... a world of happenings, not of things... The world seems to be less about objects than about interactive relationships.*
>
> – Carlo Rovelli [Seven Brief Lessons on Physics, pp. 20, 33, 43]

Here's a thought experiment: maybe our own understandings and realities ("truths"?) are not "things." Maybe our realities are more accurately understood as personal mixtures of fact and perception, refined and brought alive by rich connections with other people. Cooperative refinement is certainly involved in objective truth, which requires others to collaborate in determining what we all see in common. Scientific techniques help us refine and polish various subjective truths into tentative objective truth.

All of our realities and truths are subject to improvement, into what we might call "more perfect" understandings. They're improvable in the same way that America's founders sought a "more perfect" way of life:

> *We the People of the United States, in Order to form a more perfect Union...*   *– Preamble to the U.S. Constitution*

Social psychologist and professor of public policy Julia Minton identifies a key obstacle to 'more perfection.' She condemns echo chambers of like-minded believers and offers an exquisite, simple formula for improvement. We should listen more and argue less:

> *Because people don't want to feel what they anticipate to be unpleasant emotions, they tend to seek out media and conversation partners that support their beliefs. This tendency is called selective exposure, and it leads to echo chambers...[But] correcting... selective exposure is not very difficult... If people learn that hearing opposing views won't be as bad as they expect, we may be able to increase contact across the aisle, making our democracy healthier. Actively engaging with opposing views might make us realize that both sides have some merit... Having an accurate understanding of how people feel in conflict should help us all listen more and argue less.*   *– Julia Minton*

Ideologies

Sometimes beliefs and ideas are used to *explain* reality. At other times they aim to *change* reality, especially through political action.

In the 1790s a French Enlightenment thinker, A. L. C. Destutt de Tracy, coined the term *idéologie* to designate a 'system of ideas.' This concept was a part of his work to help explain the causes and results of the French Revolution (1789). Preceded and inspired by the American Revolution (1776), France's revolt became tragic, leading in only a few years to the Reign of Terror (1793-4). Napoleon then came to power by the late 1790s, and he criticized ideologies as being impractical – too idealistic.

In seeking to change political realities, ideologists rarely acknowledge the competing truths that undermine the purity of their cause. It's no wonder that some ideologies can have a whiff of revolution. And revolutionary fervor is not exactly known for balance and respect. Soviet dissident Aleksandr Solzhenitsyn equated ideology with illusions and lies:

> *On the day Solzhenitsyn was arrested, February, 12, 1974, he released the text of "Live Not by Lies." The next day, he was exiled to the West, where he received a hero's welcome. This moment marks the peak of his fame. Solzhenitsyn equates "lies" with ideology, the illusion that human nature and society can be reshaped to predetermined specifications.*
>
> – Ericson & Mahoney, The Solzhenitsyn Reader

As seen in their names, ideological 'systems of thought' are also known as *isms*. Most are concerned with socio-political power or group distinctions. Some examples follow, with brief clarifying descriptions:

socialism: social/economic reform through *public* ownership of property and resources; central planning

communism: *communal* control (ownership, regulation) of resources and production

capitalism: *private* property, production, investment and profit; free market economy

anarchism: belief that government is harmful and unnecessary; "anarchy" means "without authority" fascism: militaristic subordination of individuals to the nation & elites; hostile to democracy and liberalism

antifacism: (Antifa): In U.S., opposing racism and "hate groups" (such as neo-Nazis). Derived from Europe.

Naziism: (WWII Germany) "national socialism," intense nationalism dedicated to a charismatic dictator

nationalism: devotion to the nation-state (surpassing other individual, group, or global interests)

classical liberalism: = individual freedom. [New liberalism = social welfare; theological liberalism resists traditional religious authority]

conservatism: emphasizes value of traditional institutions and practices; modern conservatism advocates limited government

multiculturalism: cultural/ethnic pluralism, highlighting especially the contributions of minority cultures

environmentalism: prioritizes the quality of nature; hostile to any force or cause that harms nature

racism: judging solely on race as a determinant of status and destiny. Also obsessive race consciousness

anti-racism: opposition to people/groups perceived as racist

structural racism: anti-racist view that status disparities (wealth, housing, jobs, etc.) are attributable specifically to racism

feminism: belief in social, economic, and political equality of the sexes; boosting women's rights & interests

sexism: prejudice or discrimination based on sex *or gender*, especially against women/girls or non-binary sexuality

heterosexism: prejudice or discrimination against same-sex attraction; assumes the norm to be opposite-sex attraction

transgenderism: prejudice or discrimination against people who have changed (or want to change) gender

ableism: prejudice or discrimination based on disability

classism:	prejudice, discrimination, or imposed domination based on social, economic, or educational status
materialism:	all facts are reducible to, and caused by, *physical* materials and processes
spiritualism:	affirming reality that's *immaterial and imperceptible* by senses; contact with departed souls
mysticism:	hidden meaning thru *ecstatic/altered consciousness*, usually involving secret cultic rites
occultism:	knowledge and use of *supernatural* beings, using magic or divination (ritual, omens, etc.)
minimalism:	extreme simplicity in an art; literal, objective, unelaborated
realism:	depicting only what's actually seen (with nothing imagined)

… and more (this list is suggestive, not exhaustive).

Religions may qualify as ideologies: they too propose to explain the world and what's beyond it, though they're not always politically revolutionary. Religions usually are described more neutrally and respectfully as a "belief system" or "my faith." These are applicable especially to changing the inner life rather than laying contentious political plans. Ideology is more acutely found in religions pursuing a socio-political agenda, or in those where dogma claims certain truths to be eternal, unchanging, and unchallengeable.

Religions that demand dogmatic conformity essentially elevate collective thinking over individual conscience – another delicate balance. Collective inspiration is surely a cousin of scientific group processes, which overcome individual error in pursuit of objective truth. But we may wonder whether religious dogma reflects consensus or is imposed by an authority, arriving top-down vs. bottom-up. Science too has "experts" who claim dominion and authority over other informed opinions. Here I can't resist mentioning a favorite bumper sticker: *My karma ran over my dogma.*

So ideologies resemble ideals. Each can be seen as a superior way of understanding. Sometimes "superior" slides into "absolutely correct," reflecting the fervor and absolutism of believers. Ideologies generally can't be proven or disproven; they're not easily tested against an objective standard. Ideologies thrive because they're coherent, persuasive, and important to their followers. Consider how "heightism" isn't really an ideology because, among many human differences, it isn't considered very important (apart from basketball!). But if height was morally important, deviations in stature might be censured just as left-handedness once was. (The left side is still known as *a sinistra* in Italian and *a gauche* in French. In English translation, *sinister* and *gauche* are uncomplimentary descriptions).

Many ideologies resemble the "prejudices" we discussed in Chapter 1. They are conclusions or pre-judgments about the way things are and how we should think about them. Ideologies are not necessarily wrong, though they certainly can be.

> *An ideology, at the most fundamental level, is simply a checklist of ideas you have about the world. Having an ideology doesn't mean you've been brainwashed, it means you've come to conclusions about how the world works at some basic level… whatever word you choose, humans need limiting principles, bright lines, ideals, dogma. Bundle them together and you've got a field guide to life that helps you sift your way through new facts and data.*
>
> – Jonah Goldberg

As an example, environmentalist ideology proclaims that nothing is more important than the future of the earth, the earth is endangered, therefore… we must collapse the oil industry, mandate electric cars by X date, cancel "deniers" of these truths, etc. Feminism became the prevailing ideology of the "Me Too" movement, a critically important exposure of sexual malfeasance. Yet "Me too" produced obvious excesses, like demanding that any woman's sexual abuse claim must be believed, period, end of story. Racism, like tribalism, is a known fact of history to the present day, but historians agree that it was not (as alleged) the organizing principle or motivating purpose of the United States. We simply can't measure whether racism permeates the minds of all white Americans, including children and infants (as if such an absurd thing could be true). A 'blood guilt' allegation is pure racism, prejudging hundreds of millions as "racists" based solely on their skin color. Such judgements come with no hint of effort to examine the particular minds that are so conclusively judged.

Maybe we could start with getting to know one person rather than judging millions. But that would be slow and careful, as deliberation usually is.

Clearly, ideologies play a central role in cultural combat: they vividly capture and motivate followers. Ideologies are VERY unlikely to be changed or diminished by rival ideologies, outsiders, or alternate explanations. But an additional factor may best explain why ideologists make such wild exaggerations, and so readily take offense. Ideologies are more than moral commitments; they are *platforms* to implement a moral vision, often by imposing it on others. As we've seen, every moral value has a serious competitor, and imposing *any* ideological choice on others violates their freedom of conscience and belief.

Speaking of activism, we all seem to be independent activists now. This is according to an introduction of new features in the Internet browser Firefox. Trivialities like software colors thus aren't just an artful choice; they're products of activism. Someone else is carried away, don't you think?

Choose the color that inspires you. Independent voices can change culture. You are an Activist. You leave the world a better place than you found it and lead others to believe.

— Firefox intro to new features, 2022

Zealous ideologists can impress outsiders as fanatics – moved by excessive, unreasoning enthusiasm. Extreme conviction can push people ever further from reality as they repeatedly demand attention for their one topic, like a one-note musical instrument.

In the late 20th century a satirical magazine targeted a big newspaper that for year had described events by their unequal effects on social classes. The spoof read: *"Nuclear Bomb Exploded in New York City: Poor Hardest Hit."*

It's not easy to spot whether someone's inner reality (or "subjective truth") is well adjusted. Just two decades after devastating losses in The Great War (later called World War I), Britain's Prime Minister in 1938 sought to avoid yet another cataclysmic war. Could such devastation threaten again, so soon? Neville Chamberlain knew that battered Britain was vulnerable, especially as the U.S. still was declaring neutrality. Nevertheless, he utterly failed to see what ideological Nazi leaders were willing to do to restore Germany from its humiliation in the peace treaty after the Great War. Fortunately, Winston Churchill had distinctive experiences from much earlier British wars., and his background had taught him how to spot fanaticism:

> *Neville Chamberlain could simply not recognize pure fanaticism when he saw it up close in his visits to Berchtesgaden and Munich. Churchill, by contrast, had seen fanaticism in its Islamic fundamentalist form while soldiering on the North-West Frontier in India and in the Sudan; its tropes were familiar to him.*
>
> – Andrew Roberts

Chamberlain became known for pacifism, another "ism" that judges things through a focusing, distorting lens. Pacifists want to avoid physical violence at all costs; many refuse to support any fight. As seen in Chapter 1, that's not always well advised, especially for those with a functioning wish for liberty.

It's said that "if you only have a hammer, everything looks like a nail." Ideologies are like hammers; we defend our hammerdom with all we've got. This weakness of ideology creates a strong argument for *inductive* reasoning, working bottom up from observations and facts up to experiments and theories. The alternative seen in ideologies, *deductive* reasoning, proceeds from the top down, beginning with a committed idea and logically concluding what must follow from that "truth." Deductive (top-down) reasoning tempts us to cherry-pick evidence that supports our starting truth. Inductive (bottom-up) reasoning, the analytical mode of scientists, uses evidence gathered *without* the distorting influence of a prior commitment, which distorts what we see. Scientists reject deductive (top-down) reasoning because it begins with an answer rather than observations. This priority for abstract answers is the analytical mode of ideologies and belief systems:

Historian John Lukacs urged students to grapple with historical facts and people, not abstractions. In this way, Lukacs argues against those who imbue the past with their own pet ideas, cutting to the core of so many isms, Marxism first among them, that claim to understand humanity's past, present and destiny. – Mario Smith

A French thinker of the mid-20th century said that speculative reasoning, which lacks observations or data, causes our most significant errors. Rather than reasoning through 'what must be true' or 'how it must be' based on some ideology or other prior reasoning, our best bet is to see anew for ourselves, like scientists:

The great human error is to reason in place of finding out. – Simone Weil

***

Expectations

"…and they lived happily ever after." Not.

Hopes, wishes, and fairy tales profoundly shape our views of what's possible. Any of us would dearly love to be permanently, perfectly happy along with our closest friends and family. But anyone who expects this – with never a setback, lag, or lapse – hasn't had a long relationship. You'd think that second marriages would involve more realistic attitudes and subdued fantasies. But statistics say these marriages produce even higher divorce rates. Wishful thinking is based in emotional weaknesses and logical failures that lead us to mix too much hope into our expectations:

> *Misplaced expectations are the root of all disappointment.*
>
> – Jim Miley, Crossroads Professional Coaching

> *Instead of being disappointed with an outcome, we really should be disappointed in our own unrealistic expectations. We can ask for things but we don't always get them.*
>
> – Bradley Foster, Giant Steps Coaching

A clever definition of happiness says it is *results divided by expectations.* Paupers with low expectations can be happy, while billionaires with galaxy-scale expectations can be miserable. Philosophers discuss whether a half-full glass represents a good drink or a bad fill – though any amount could satisfy, depending on our expectations. Religions teach gratitude for what we have, forgiveness in what we lack, and humility about what we deserve. A profound understanding of wealth is that it has no number or dimension. Rather than large, impressive accumulations, wealth is simply knowing that you do (and will) have what you need. The rest is wayward expectation.

A husband has described how his terrific wife embraces humility, and accepts personal responsibility for her expectations:

When asked how to successfully raise four kids, my wife says "I just lower my expectations!" It's the key to happiness. – Wes Trochlil

Unmet expectations can lead to destructive behaviors that ruin lives. One such expectation is the American belief that each generation should have, and is owed a standard of living better than the last:

[Many opioid victims feel] betrayed by the world... overdoses, suicides, and alcohol abuse are the results of "cumulative distress," or the overall "failure of life to turn out as expected."
– Olga Khazan, Atlantic Magazine

Expectations shape us. Expecting little or nothing minimizes letdowns...

Blessed is he who expects nothing, for he shall never be disappointed.
– Jonathan Swift

...while imagining the best outcome supports ambition and achievement:

I always have to dream up there against the stars. If I don't dream I will make it, I won't even get close. – Henry J. Kaiser

Perfection is not attainable, but if we chase perfection we can catch excellence. – Vince Lombardi

Ah, but a man's reach should exceed his grasp, Or what's a heaven for?
- Robert Browning

Yet there's a huge gap between dreams, perfection, or heaven compared to *what we actually need.* An old cliché says to *expect* the worst but work like hell for the best. Been there, done that. But that cliché is still great advice for managing expectations, which drive us mad when they're out of control.

***

112

Let's return to love and marriage – that "ever after" thing. Love is a top subject in popular entertainment, presented in endless variations that rarely dull our appetite for more. This is a great testament to our universal need for companionship, and for love if we can have it. But amid all those powerful themes of hope and joy, longing and loneliness, lament and loss, one potent lyric squarely faces the *simultaneous* presence of flaws mixed with occasional feelings of perfection:

> *You can be flawed enough, but perfect for another person,*
> *Someone who will be there for you when you fall apart.*
> *Guiding your direction when you're riding through the dark*
> *Oh that's you and me.*   – lyric, You + Me:
> Alecia Moore (P!nk) and Dallas Greene

Marriages, or any style of intimate committed relationships, are multi-layered liaisons with umpteen roles. Some roles are necessary and others are probable, including: spouse, lover, friend, soulmate, life partner, sounding board, advisor, fulfillment provider, anchor, co-parent, errand runner, chore sharer, problem solver, ally, compatible travel companion, co-planner, accomplice, encourager, motivator, caring critic, protector, caretaker/nurse, chef, etc. Simply spinning out this list should convince us that one person can never consistently and forever fill all these parts. Still less could anyone do most of them well, or any one of them perfectly.

Some of us marry while imagining that bliss can last forever. But we realize – in our deepest recesses, if not our full awareness – that ideals aren't realities. Germany's great poet Johann Goethe has some fun with this:

> *Love is an ideal thing, marriage a real thing; a confusion of the real*
> *with the ideal never goes unpunished.*
>
>   – Johann Wolfgang von Goethe, *The Cynic's Lexicon*

We think of perfection as something without defect, weakness, or blemish – clearly an unreachable abstraction. A "perfectionist" – someone always working to get better – is more accurately described as an improver, an improvist, or some similar word not yet invented. The lack of nouns for a persistent, gritty, but imperfect person reveals our confusion over what perfect means. Yet "perfection" is indeed a powerful way to describe our intense gratification when imperfect people fit together so splendidly. Perfection is an emotional word, not so much a logical one.

Though love in practice isn't perfect, clearly it can be beautiful. This view has been wonderfully expressed by an anonymous American woman, describing her kaleidoscopic expectations about what love is and isn't:

I've always wanted to be loved. Everyone does, I guess – though there are some people who won't admit it. And I suppose no one really understands what love is...I know I don't. When I was younger, I had some romantic fantasies about love. I could be found by a handsome young man, and he'd sweep me away and protect me and take care of me, and I'd simply adore him. But life isn't that way. And I've since come to realize that it's only a little childlike part of me that wants to be loved in that way. I've known some people who have been swept away and protected and taken care of. I know what that can do to people – especially to women...I might like to play at it now and then, but in reality the idea sickens me.

Sometimes I'd have the passing thought of a romance where all the ardor and vitality and excitement of that other kind of love existed, but on a mutual level. We'd sweep each other away, protect and take care of each other. That's more acceptable, but life really isn't like that either. At least not for long... You start recognizing that each of you has feet of clay... Sooner or later you realize that what you loved was an image of the other person...They start to weigh you

114

down...it simply burns you out...and you want to go looking for someone else, someone new who will fit your image of an ideal lover.

Then there's the kind of love that means staying with another person: sharing your life, putting up with each other's difficulties and stupidities, being willing to accept them as they are without demanding that they change to fit your fantasies... just hanging in there with each other because...that's what you both want. You just see things through with each other, weather things, plug away at life...sometimes things come up between you that make big trouble. But you just hang in there...

It's like the love you have for your children. Not quite the same, but it has the same steady constancy... the love that goes on underneath the fights and the pains and the little pleasures that you get... it just keeps going, like nothing in the world could ever destroy it.

But... I've always felt there's something more as well...there are times when love seems to separate itself off from all the things you do with or for someone else, when it takes on a sort of presence of its own...it's like you can sense it all around you, as if you're in it rather than it being in you. It's hard to describe, but sometimes I just know it's there, all around me and in me and through me. That's what real love is, and I don't understand it at all. I just know that it's not a people thing. It includes everything... It's just so incredibly beautiful ... This is the deepest meaning of being "in" love.

– from Gerald G. May, M.D., *Will and Spirit*

***

Let's say that we've found a marvelous peace and balance about what's possible and what isn't. How then do we deal with the deceptions that constantly creep into our thinking about realities and wishes?

Balancing Idealism and Reality

1. List your dearest hopes and wishes. Then find examples of how wishful thinking about those ideals may have distorted your sense of reality.
2. Which ideologies are you committed to?
3. What new information (or refuted old info) would change your beliefs?
4. In thinking about your expectations, which are you proud of (or ashamed of)? Which might benefit from a little realistic polishing, or an idealistic boost?
5. What are your prejudices? Don't pretend you have none; remember, these are pre-judgments about the way things are. Now, which of your prejudices are constructive? Which might be trouble?
6. Think of the experiences and influences that shaped who you uniquely are, and what you believe. Which of your subjective truths might differ most from the objective truth that a scientific process might find? In other words, what aspects of *your* reality are least likely to be shared by others?

Further Reading

Kate Bowler	Everything Happens for a Reason: And Other Lies I've Loved
Kate Bowler	No Cure for Being Human (And Other Truths I Need to Hear)
Thomas Sowell	A Conflict of Visions
Kahneman, Sibony, & Sunstein	Noise
Telmo Pievani	Imperfection
Andres Newman	Fracture
Frank S. Frick	A Journey Through the Hebrew Scriptures
Martin Seligman	various works on positive psychology
Thomas Sowell	Conflict of Visions

Chapter 3 – Honesty, Deception

*People do not believe lies because they have to but because
they want to.* – Malcolm Muggeridge

*When you want to help people, you tell them the truth. When you want
to help yourself, you tell them what they want to hear.* – Thomas Sowell

*There is a peace that settles within us when we look steadily at the truth,
not pretending life is something it is not.* – Kate Bowler

For over two centuries, millions of Americans have heard a well-known story about George Washington's honesty. In 1806 a posthumous biographer wrote that Washington as a small child was given a hatchet; soon his father was angrily accusing him of chopping down a tree. George exclaimed:

> *Father, I cannot tell a lie: I did cut the tree with my hatchet.*
>
> — attributed to George Washington

Historians believe this story is factually untrue. It appeared in print about seven years after Washington's death, and nearly seventy years after his alleged burst of virtue. The story *symbolized* Washington's outstanding character, but probably misrepresented his actual history. If we define honesty as being "not deceitful" – and if we accept that Washington was a man of integrity – is the story deceptive history or symbolic truth?

A similar pattern applies to Jesus. Virtually everything known about his earthly life was written 50+ years after his death by people who didn't know or observe him. Their accounts appear to include many statements of the imagination, like virtually all ancient scriptures or stories. Historical writing was only several hundred years old. Chronicles could

117

be infused with theological ideas, a typical way that the ancients understood cause and effect. Theological explanations were common especially after sudden reversals of fortune, which *demand* answers about causes: earthquakes, an enemy's collapse, a child's death, deliverance from famine, or a brutal execution of an inspiring religious leader.

The Scientific Revolution was about 1500 years into the future. Magical accounts explained things that had no other explanation. Now with 2000 years of hindsight, we might ask: is it fair to characterize very old stories as honest or deceptive? *Were* they 'true,' and if so to whom, in what way? To express all these questions differently: do standards of truth, honesty, and/or deception change from millennium to millennium, or day to day?

You may be thinking: is there really a tradeoff here? Honesty is nearly always good, deception rarely is. **What decent person would choose deception? As we'll convincingly see, deception is rampantly common. It's even occasionally good.**

We deceive not so much because we're dishonest; we lie because we so strongly affirm what we WANT to be true. We believe these wishful things intentionally, despite doubts. In a sense we *deceive ourselves* most of all; we drink our own kool-aid, so to speak. Inevitably we're forced to choose between our comfortable, questionable beliefs and uncomfortable, truer ones. Otherwise we cannot improve. And if there's no room for improvement, we're either perfect or dead. Each of us is sub-optimal.

Come to think of it – do we *today* have a clear, workable understanding of *what is a lie*? Many of us don't. Answering that question is a first step in more clearly understanding what truth is, and how we can live it.

What are Lies?

Let's start with the bold accusation: *"Liar!"* It oozes contempt for a lie, and especially for the liar. It powerfully announces the accuser's hostility about what's been said. "Liar!" is a *relational* term masquerading as a fact; it takes a credibility problem and turns it into a character insult. Though many lies involve at least two people (and thus are relational), we do well to remember that we easily deceive ourselves. We often bask in our self-compliment rather than acknowledging a less flattering truth.

A simple, short definition of a lie is an *"intentional deception."* We'll be seeing how a great deal of nuance is packed in those two words.

A Boeing Chief Pilot once misled FAA regulators about pilot training for the 737 MAX flight control system, which later was blamed for two crashes. After the disasters the Chief pleaded ignorance, saying he hadn't been told about engineering changes that impaired flight control. He described his misinformed statements to regulators as lies:

> *So I basically lied to the regulators (unknowingly).*
> – Mark Forkner, former Boeing 737 MAX Chief Technical Pilot

Forkner's mistaken statements indeed were deceptive, but they weren't *intentionally* deceptive – so they weren't lies. Sometimes people flippantly say "I lied" after realizing they've spoken in error. But mistakes, accidents, and poor communications are not lies; deception was not *intended* in such cases. A lie is usually a betrayal of integrity, never a mistake.

A more nuanced, rigorous definition is "a *false statement deliberately presented as true.*" Here a statement must be made, thus excluding silent deceptions (such as quietly allowing a misunderstanding to continue). Think of a husband who loses a job, fails to tell his wife, but never says he remains employed. He said nothing, but his inaction intentionally deceives.

According to our second definition, his behavior is not a lie because there's no false *statement*. But it is a lie of intentional deception.

A yet more complicated definition of a lie is "an *assertion that the speaker believes to be false.* This condemns a statement *intended* to deceive even if it turns out to be true. Think of a golfer on a home course, advising a guest to be foolishly aggressive on a quirky hole... but then the strategy wins the hole. The host intended to mislead, but instead helped an opponent win. Our third definition says he lied because he *intended to deceive*; our first definition says he didn't lie because he didn't *actually deceive* his guest into bad play.

Defining a lie in only two words, *intentional deception,* captures most violations of truthful integrity, without all the fuss. The two-word version is most easily remembered and applied, so it's the definition we'll use. **A lie is an *intentional deception,*** and it may involve no words at all.

Words like "candor" and "frankness" hint that concealment and evasion are common. A friend who says "Candidly, Mike," "Frankly, Mike" then "Honestly, Mike" eventually makes Mike wonder about reliability. Conversations are about much more than truth: we want to impress, hide weaknesses, emphasize pros and downplay cons. A famed songwriter and singer was once asked why a play about his life made him "scared:"

Being found out is the scariest thing... because we all have this façade... I'm not some big star. I'm just me. – Neil Diamond

We all want to persuade, to make a sale, to entertain with tall tales – or simply to be liked. So we're highly tempted to bend and shape the truth. As we'll explore in more depth, lies are not always bad. We may even *virtuously deceive* someone if we're pursuing another moral good, such as preventing harm, preserving privacy, or protecting secrets.

Many of our conversations conceal much more than we realize, and sometimes that's appropriate. Full transparency can cause big problems. We generally want to hide information that could be misused, especially as technology makes data more easily exposed and spread. Some people push for transparency laws to identify political contributors – including addresses – that could expose donors to potential harassment. Exposed parade routes, itineraries, and schedules for public appearances are ripe for an enemy to exploit. Battle plans or intelligence reports are even more sensitive. The need for secrecy is obvious, yet in a democracy spying is uniquely challenged. Who should oversee the spies when the government is ultimately accountable to the people? More generally: in a free society, *who should judge* how we protect sensitive information?

The founder of C-SPAN has recalled what motivated him in 1979 to create a broadcast network dedicated to live coverage of the U.S. Congress:

> *Lying is the word that I would use to describe this town. I don't know if it will ever stop. It's gotten worse than getting better, and both sides do it. You've got to listen very carefully to what they're saying.... People in this town often ask for "transparency." I don't even like the word: It's used all the time. They don't really believe it.*
>
> *– Brian Lamb*

When it comes to balancing transparency, concealment, and simply lying, we think the serious offenders are the other guys. "I'm good, they're bad," at least usually. But that's not nearly accurate. Deceptions are common among people of all types; only a few are evil betrayals we all condemn. Here we're interested in the gray areas, the vast little deceptions of daily life. To paraphrase Jerry Lee Lewis, rock & roll's early wild man: *there's a whole lotta foolin' going on*. If you're not yet convinced, you soon will be.

***

MAD, a popular satire magazine for teenagers, was published 1952 - 2019. At its peak in the 1970s, millions of teenagers were reading it. One reader grew into a Pulitzer-awarded cartoonist who fondly remembered MAD's irreverent tone and how it shaped his young worldview:

> *Mad was, 'the entire adult world is lying to you, and we are part of the adult world. Good luck to you.' I think that shaped my entire generation.* — Art Spiegelman

To emphasize once again, deceiving others is rampant, yet much of our fooling is *self*-deception and it's as pernicious as deceiving others. A key factor that shields us from truth – from learning, correcting, growing, and diminishing disputes – is our runaway commitment to reinforcing *what we already believe*. And that's not nearly the same thing as the truth.

Why we tend to affirm what we already believe

Believed lies have a simple, common characteristic. They support our interests and beliefs. Human nature's blinkered quality is captured in the aphorism "none are so blind as those who will not see." Consider five keen minds that observed this aspect of human behavior over a 2000-year period:

> *Men in general are quick to believe that which they wish to be true.*
> — Julius Caesar

> *The time is coming when people won't listen to good teaching. Instead, they will look for teachers who will please them by telling them only what they are itching to hear.*
> — 2nd Timothy 4:3, by an anonymous author ca 100 AD

> *Man prefers to believe what he prefers to be true.*— Francis Bacon

People only see what they are prepared to see.

– Ralph Waldo Emerson

People do not believe lies because they have to but because they want to.

– Malcolm Muggeridge

Psychologists call this **confirmation bias** – our strong orientation toward beliefs that confirm we're right or good. We want to think well of ourselves, so we select information accordingly. Confirmation bias moves us to accept any information that supports our hopes:

It isn't hard to convince somebody you love them if you know what they want to hear. – Joe Goldberg, a character in the TV series 'You'

We favor information that confirms our wants and needs, a process called **motivated reasoning**. Rather than using balanced judgment to make an impartial decision – which many of us *believe to be* our standard operating procedure – we typically choose evidence to support existing beliefs, commitments, or advantages. When we hear an argument for a favored cause, we sort through it for *reasons to agree*. Upon hearing about a disfavored cause, we scan for *reasons to escape*. Our reasoning is highly influenced by a subconscious compulsion to defend our prior beliefs:

The reasoning process is more like a lawyer defending a client than a judge or scientist seeking the truth. – Jonathan Haidt

When our beliefs are threatened, we hunger for evidence, reasons, and stories to confirm we've been right. Our brains' first job is to confirm that our understandings are reliably right and true, so we'll be more successful.

Self-criticism is so much rarer. Few of us welcome the conclusion that we're weak or wrong. Psychologists have demonstrated that we're far from impartial or balanced in this regard.

We're biased to see ourselves in a positive light. We want to believe that we're rational and smart. We recall our past actions as more sensible than they were. We also give ourselves too much credit and don't remember our mistakes as well as we do our successes.

– Professor Deborah Small

Intelligent, educated people are even better at self-deceptive rationalizing. The Danish literary folktale *The Emperor's New Clothes* tells of an innocent child who exclaims "The Emperor has no clothes!" while all the adults pretend otherwise. The child's eyes aren't better. His mind is simply uncluttered by the fear of consequences, pretensions, self-deceptions, and the powers of motivated reasoning so commonly found among adults. Especially smart ones.

The great scientist who analyzed uranium's decay into lead (and discovered the earth's age) also pioneered 20th century scientific efforts against lead poisoning from auto fuel. He saw his scientific gift in exactly these terms – of seeing 'naked emperors' in the falsehoods that others accept:

I'm a little child. You know the emperor's new clothes? I can see the naked emperor, just because I'm a little child-minded person. I'm not smart. I mean, good scientists are like that. They have the minds of children, to see through all this façade.

– Clair Patterson

Aleksandr Solzhenitsyn, an anti-Soviet dissident, made a similar point in his 1974 essay, *Live Not by Lies*. Soviet citizens frequently lied to themselves about their own responsibility – their complicity – in accepting government falsehoods about their degraded situation. Solzhenitsyn said the only way to resist is to refuse participation in the everyday deceptions required to survive in their Communist society.

We lie to ourselves to preserve our peace of mind. It is not they who should be blamed but ourselves... we can see that the young and presumptuous people who thought they would make our country just and happy through terror, bloody rebellion and civil war were themselves misled... personal non-participation in lies is the easiest thing to do and most destructive for the lies. Because when people renounce lies it cuts short [the lie's] existence. Like a virus, [lies] can survive only in a living organism. – Aleksandr Solzhenitsyn

Solzhenitsyn's powerful yet simple solution requires no shouting or violence. It's even easier than the civil disobedience practiced by Henry David Thoreau, Mohandas Gandhi, and Martin Luther King:

Let us refuse to say what we do not think... If we did not paste together the dead bones and scales of ideology, if we did not sew together rotting rags, we would be astonished at how quickly the lies would be rendered helpless and would subside...Let us make a choice: whether to remain consciously a servant of falsehood (of course, it is not out of inclination, but [rather] to feed one's family, that one raises one's children in the spirit of lies), or to shrug off the lies and become an honest man worthy of respect from one's children and contemporaries. – Aleksandr Solzhenitsyn

Solzhenitsyn doesn't use the term "motivated reasoning." But he speaks eloquently about how we deceive ourselves, feeding our emotional needs by hiding from unpleasant truth. Solzhenitsyn himself needed to keep a job, so he could provide food and warmth for his family.

Daily living brings spin, propaganda, half-truths, veiling lies, satire, hype, casual exaggeration, derisive jokes, sarcasm, fake news, metaphors, myths, misinformation, wishful thinking, fantasies, illusions, and pretense. All of these qualify as "false" in some sense, yet we believe many of them.

The next time you have an argument or a 'vigorous discussion,' watch for your own motivated reasoning to spill forth. Reflexive, subconscious urges distort our reasoning in order to defend our beliefs, retain our self-respect, and secure essential needs like food, love, and social respect. Motivated reasoning races to the forefront, especially in fight mode. This happened for me earlier today, yesterday, and the day before that... and probably for you as well, all unnoticed. If I weren't writing about it, this morning's motivated reasoning may have slipped my own attention. Every reader of this paragraph has resisted challenges to his or her most deeply cherished values, such as equality, independence, loyalty, or honesty. Each of these values are subject to trade-offs, and must be balanced with competing priorities. Author Julia Galef describes motivated reasoning in a way that acknowledges the competition between various ideas and values:

[Motivated reasoning is] trying to make some ideas win, and others lose; [it is] the drive to attack or defend ideas. – Julia Galef

This mentality is like that of an embattled lawyer or soldier. An alternative is the "scout mindset," which suspends judgment and seeks impartial truth about what's really out there. A scout is curious and treasures discoveries – especially if in the process they overturn an illusion or a misunderstanding. The soldier and scout mindsets are metaphors for how each of us process information in our daily lives. Unfortunately, most of think and behave like the soldiers:

Our judgment is just strongly inclined, unconsciously, by which side we want to win. This is ubiquitous, and what's scary is how unconscious it is. A soldier's mindset is rooted in the need to protect yourself and your side and to defeat the enemy. In contrast, a scout tries to get an accurate picture of reality, even when that's unpleasant or inconvenient... Scouts are more likely to say that it's virtuous to test your own beliefs. Their self-worth isn't tied to how right or wrong they are about a particular topic. If new information contradicts their beliefs, they say 'I might be wrong... and that doesn't mean I'm bad or stupid.' Having good judgment, making accurate predictions, and making good decisions is mostly about which mindset you're in.   – Julia Galef

As our beliefs and convictions jump to the front of the line, evidence and reason *sometimes* follow. But they rarely challenge what we've already concluded. Such challenges would threaten our sense of identity, our world view, and our social status among like-minded people.

To go against the dominant thinking of your friends, of most of the people you see every day, is perhaps the most difficult act of heroism you can perform.   – Theodore H. White

Reasoned conclusions harden into convictions, which we defend fiercely.

Convictions are more dangerous foes of truth than lies.
    – Friedrich Nietzsche

We turn political disagreements into bitter contests of unshakable ideals. Yet all of us have been disappointed, at least occasionally, when a highly favored belief, cause, or candidate turns out to be less right or good than we thought. We have been deceived, or we deceived ourselves. Either of these can be tough to admit, especially self-deception or naivete:

To become disillusioned, you must earlier have been illusioned.
    – Paul Fussell

Being illusioned is comfortable, sometimes even necessary or justified. Many surviving women of Pol Pot's killing fields in Cambodia had witnessed the starvation, murder, and decapitation of their husbands and children. When they became blind, doctors found nothing physically wrong with their eyes or nervous systems. Their "functional blindness" was linked to psychological factors. Who could blame the women (or their subconscious minds) for "choosing" blindness? A reality like that cries out for escape, even at the expense of truth.

For these women, impaired sight **relieves suffering.** This is an obvious and common reason to embrace lies and illusions. We might think of lies as a category of blindness that we willfully choose:

> *We create the illusions we need to go on. And one day, when they no longer dazzle or comfort, we tear them down, brick by glittering brick, until we are left with nothing but the bright light of honesty. The light is liberating. Necessary. Terrifying. We stand naked and emptied before it. And when it is too much for our eyes to take, we build a new illusion to shield us from its relentless truth.*
>
> – Libba Bray

We may think that truth and honesty are our highest priorities or virtues. But evading suffering – or simply surviving – will prevail in most cases. Stories of those who suffer or die for their understanding of truth – like Socrates, Jesus, and Thomas More – have been retold for hundreds or thousands of years. Their stories are memorable and admirable, precisely because they're profound exceptions to expected human behavior.

***

Specific Reasons We Deceive Selves and Others

Generally speaking, it's a moral failing to intentionally deceive, to lie. But sometimes deceptions are good and commendable! Let's take a look at some categories where lying is beneficial.

Benevolence and Consolation

Consider a mortally wounded person: the last words (s)he may hear are *"everything is going to be alright."* Benevolent lies calm a frightened child, or settle a panicked adult who is very much in danger. We elevate a child's joy and imagination with stories of Santa Claus, or promises of a reward from the Tooth Fairy. We groom children's capacity to tame fear by telling stories of dragons and monsters. We instill morals through fables and fairy tales. When we adults receive an unwelcome gift, soon to be trashed or regifted, we thank the giver to protect his feelings or to return goodwill. Speaking candidly in these situations is called 'brutal honesty' for good reason. We usually choose other words that extend care and avoid harm.

Most of us would have few qualms about deceiving someone who invades our privacy, or seems to be probing for a weakness to exploit. Think of a disruptive phone call: we're likely to defend our time and attention with a lie that gets us off the phone. At other times we might hide a hurtful truth with kindly *evasion*. If we silently avoid the subject, we can stop short of being explicitly deceptive:

In some situations, forgiveness and staying silent may be more gracious than speaking an unkind truth. – Brian Carpenter

Diversions and evasions are passive. If they fail, a more active "white lie" avoids harm or embarrassment, or keeps a secret (e.g., about a surprise party). Lies that benefit others are called altruistic, benevolent, or "prosocial" lies. A prospective date suddenly "remembers" that her grandmother will be visiting this Saturday. We similarly "remember" some excuse when a nagging salesman asks repeatedly for an appointment. "Butler lies" misstate our availability when we want to avoid somebody (*Jim is on another call; can he call you back?*). In a way, such lies are a kindness, substituting a gentle letdown for a bluntly honest rejection (*You're an obnoxious pest and Jim wants nothing to do with you*). Butler lies have become far more common in 'always on' social media, where unavailability feels to some like abandonment. Butler lies are common on dating sites, where users fudge not only their availability but also their weight, height, and other details to appear more desirable. White lies and butler lies are *active* deceptions. Yet few of us spend much energy condemning the little fibs that diminish conflict, reduce suffering, or induce joy. We tell protective or benevolent lies to achieve a greater purpose. Many who *hear* those pleasing lies prefer them to the truth.

Of course, there's a flip side. When we use lies to reduce pain, we cover up an important signal (as with anger or regret) that change is needed. Hiding from unpleasant truths – like symptoms of tightness in the chest, or a suspicion that 'something's just not right' – can be costly or fatal. Sugarcoating weaknesses or threats can ease our minds, but it also postpones change, maybe until it's too late. If we downplay risk to others, they may not be careful enough; overplaying risk can create a bunker mentality. When we don't really know the real risk, it can seem impossible to choose between warning or downplaying.

Most of all, deceiving others may work for a short while, but eventually it undermines their trust and confidence. As Abe Lincoln said, *you cannot fool all of the people all the time*, and that includes ourselves. Self-deception can boost self-confidence and distort perceived reality for a while, maybe even vaulting us to great destinations in a risky venture. It also can send us crashing into the rocks we've pretended not to see.

Failure and Success

As the saying has it, repeating a behavior and expecting a different outcome is the definition of insanity. But repeating efforts with a good outcome is called persistence. We praise the diligent, then say they're "definitely insane" after failures. Multiple visits in swimwear to a winter-blown Arctic coastline is insanity, and repeated falls while learning to ride a bicycle is persistence, because in each case we know the likely outcome. Yet much of the time we're unable to predict a result and must decide in advance what's persistent and what's insane. This situation is ripe for self-deception.

Dreamers since antiquity have dreamed of human flight. They failed and died repeatedly until the Wright Brothers succeeded in 1903. Thomas Edison was said to have failed 1,000 or more times before inventing the light bulb. When asked how that felt, he supposedly said:

> *I didn't fail 1,000 times. The light bulb was an invention of 1,000 steps.*
> – Thomas Edison

In another version, Edison claims many more failures, each one a success:

> *I have not failed 10,000 times. I have successfully found 10,000 ways that will not work.* – Thomas Edison

Can an undefeated outlook be justified only in the rear-view mirror? Wouldn't we think very differently immediately after that 9,999[th] failure, based on information available at the time? Would we be *deceiving ourselves* to grittily believe a 10,000[th] Arctic beach visit will be pleasant?

Investor Warren Buffett and his partner Charlie Munger have built astounding fortunes in part by studying human folly, including self-deception. Common mistakes by investors include allowing hope to triumph over experience, or using old ideas that don't fit new circumstances:

The ability to destroy your ideas rapidly instead of slowly when the occasion is right is one of the most valuable things. You have to work hard on it… It's bad to have an opinion you're proud of if you can't state the arguments for the other side better than your opponents. This is a great mental discipline.   – Charlie Munger

Self-deception probably dwarfs other forms of lying for a simple reason: **people are poor critics of their own thinking**. This is the principle behind peer review for scientific papers, committee review, and consulting in teams. The physicist and Nobel prize winner Richard Feynman said this vulnerability is very serious for scientists, who must avoid close-minded self-regard, flattery, or pride if they're to have any chance of discovering truth. Yet the principle applies to all of us:

*The first principle is that **you must not fool yourself** - and you are the easiest person to fool.*   – Richard Feynman

In victory we credit our own marvelous abilities. In failure we blame the circumstances or other people. Some players see fairness only if they've won; a loss means the game was rigged. These are examples of *motivated reasoning* in pure form: we interpret outcomes to shed the best light on our experiences, abilities, and worthiness.

For nearly forty years I retold the story of witnessing Boston College quarterback Doug Flutie throw his famous hail-Mary pass to win a big football game just as time expired. I was there for one of the most memorable moments in college football history! Except that I wasn't, as I discovered from an account of Flutie's play in a Florida bowl game. I had attended a game near Boston, then saw that Florida pass on TV a week or two later. I saw it repeatedly in replays over the years; my "mind's eye" convinced me that my real eyes "witnessed" something they hadn't. Even a trivial memory can be distorted by self-serving bias. Our persistent self-regard and self-interest are among the root causes for why we deceive:

> *Victory has a thousand fathers; defeat is an orphan.*
>
> – popularized by John F. Kennedy

I know failure. Working for decades in entrepreneurial ventures, failure constantly loomed. It occurred uncomfortably often, small and large. Given the high failure rate of new businesses, entrepreneurship may simply require a strong dose of self-deception about the odds, though it's usually called optimism, creative disruption, and enthusiasm. For many like me, it's the only way to live: **to try**. It's a strategy to avoid reaching life's end and wondering what might have happened if I had enough courage to risk. For me, a secondary consideration – in *distant* second place – would be whether I've deceived myself or struggled needlessly.

Grief, Escape, and Fear

Consider the experience of grief. Bereaved survivors grasp for consolations. We may be told that "there's a reason for everything"… that misfortune is a punishment for past misdeeds, and our suffering is deserved. These consolations are welcome explanations for some, as Elaine Pagels explained in our discussion of ideals. Many misfortunes have no grand reason or cause that explains them. Grief is a ripe opportunity for wishful thinking.

It shocks us when someone speaks ill of the recently deceased. It violates a custom of remembering someone's virtues, and few if any shortcomings. In these situations, 'brutal honesty' borders on cruelty. Yet grief counselors know that comforting words are secondary. A grieving survivor will remember the simple *presence* of friends long after their supportive words have faded. Nevertheless, the bereaved or seriously ill sometimes insist on tough honesty, even if it's just silence that refuses easy, wishful answers:

Do not tell me there will be a blessing in the breaking, that it will ever be a grace... that what does not kill me will make me stronger, that this will make me stronger... or more compassionate... or more grateful for what I had... or that God will not send me more than I can bear. Give me instead the blessing of sitting with me when you cannot think of what to say.

– Jan Richardson

Suffering people often seek to escape their plight by denials or wishmaking. But courageously facing unpleasant truths can bring quiet rewards:

There is a peace that settles within us when we look steadily at the truth, not pretending life is something it is not.

– Kate Bowler

We console our fearful selves with optimistic lies. We divert fear and despair as failure looms. Optimism before failure will be seen later as a delusion. The same optimism before escaping a disaster will be seen as 'darkness before the dawn.' Pessimists can avoid trouble by acting on their dark forebodings, yet they defeat themselves by quitting before they begin. Pessimists predict more disasters than actually occur. Whether today's prediction is a hope or a delusion depends on the unpredictable future – yet we must act (or not act) based on some outlook or vision of the future.

Sometimes we tell ourselves that a problem is unsolvable, when in truth we lack courage to confront uncomfortable facts. Think of a co-worker's poor work performance, a friend's boorishness, or a spouse's emotional distance: they linger on when we don't address the problem. Even *positive* feelings can remain bottled up when we feel vulnerable (as when we're stressed to say "I love you" for the first time). But until that's done, an intimate partner may misperceive a paramour's true feelings. So we hide, pretend, evade, or lie, all to avoid the awkward unease that honesty can cause.

People assume that honest conversations will be personally distressing and harm *their relationships. In reality, honesty is much more enjoyable and less harmful for relationships than people anticipate. The more people practice honesty, the more they will realize that their predictions about its negative consequences are wrong. People can also practice delivering honesty in more palatable ways, for example, by clearly stating their good intentions before delivering difficult or critical information.*

– Emma Levine, professor of behavioral science

Psychologists describe an "action crisis" when there's a breaking point. That's when poor results continue to pile on while we want to keep trying. At this point outside opinions can really help: friends or counsellors may better read the tea leaves long before we do. Annie Duke, a specialist in behavioral science, suggests making a list of "kill criteria" – benchmarks for when to quit, determined in advance when objectivity is higher. These can powerfully guide us when emotions later rage and judgment is questionable. For Duke, whose book *Quit* examines this problem at length, persistence is harmful when we're riding the wrong horse into the future:

Success does not lie in sticking to things. It lies in picking the <u>right thing</u> to stick to, and quitting the rest.

– Annie Duke

One technique for calling it a day is to ask yourself: "do I get energy out of doing this?" Nobody wants to abandon a goal just before the sun will rise on it. But the never-ending darkness of chasing unattainable goals brings serious costs. We miss chances to win elsewhere, and anxiety dysregulates our bodies. High levels of the stress hormone cortisol can trigger inflammation and some clinical diseases. Exhaustion, sadness, irritability, and depression are among other clues that a reckoning is in order.

The adaptive part of quitting isn't about just letting go whenever there's an obstacle. It's about being able to let go when there's no pathway to success anymore.

– Dr. Carsten Wrosch, professor of psychology

Fiction and Entertainment

Imaginative stories are a powerful way to take risks in the abstract, to explore what *could be.* They broaden our experience virtually. An irony of fiction is that we read stories to find "truths" that may have little to do with scientific or physical facts. Great fiction conveys psychological, spiritual, or relational truth that may even contradict literal or historic truths:

Stories can be true whether they happened or not.

– Barbara Brown Taylor

Fiction is well equipped to explore the intangible, the immeasurable, or the transcendent. Think of hope, love, dreams, awe, friendship, forgiveness, gratitude, or yearning. All are literally untouchable.

Historical accounts trade heavily in such intangibles or they're just dry ledgers of dates and events. Standards are slippery for what we should consider historical truth. We've seen how George Washington's biographer tucked an imaginative character sketch into his childhood. Almost two centuries later, Edmund Morris's 1999 biography, *Dutch: A Memoir of Ronald Reagan,* used imaginary characters and events to conjure Reagan's notoriously elusive personality. Many critics didn't appreciate Morris's mixture of fact and fiction, which uncomfortably mixing standards for truth.

Imaginary dialogue in historical dramas can convey essential truths even if the specific words were never spoken. *The Crown,* a widely admired TV production about Britain's royal family, covers decades of historical events that simply weren't recorded when they happened. The show's creator hints that even if a detailed transcript were to miraculously appear, strict accuracy could mislead, whereas artistic license might better capture truths.

I'm not entirely persuaded that accuracy is a virtue in itself. Television is an interpretive and creative medium… if I felt that, at the expense of an inaccuracy I was somehow violating an underlying truth, then I couldn't live with that. So you get into this accuracy versus truth thing.
— Peter Morgan, creator/writer, *The Crown*

A great American author made a similar point, bluntly:

A historian who would convey the truth must lie. Often he must enlarge the truth by diameters, otherwise his reader would not be able to see it. — Mark Twain

Any whale watching veteran knows that a giant leap, as seen in TV ads, is rare or non-existent for normal observers. Seeing a brief tail flip a few feet above the water, from ¼ mile away for 2-3 seconds, is great luck. For kids who've seen Disney's *Finding Nemo,* a real aquarium looks diluted. Thrilling events in nature are spaced days, months, or decades apart. Instant replays, year-end summaries, legislative reviews, postmortem analyses, digests, and news media accounts concentrate reality into a package that's more interesting and stimulating than a live experience. Actors and literature give us heightened, intensified versions of ourselves.

Figurative language in the arts (and even in political rhetoric) moves us emotionally in a way that literal, realistic words do not. The power of a ship commander saying *all hands on deck* soars above other word choices (like *everybody go outside).* Saying *the pen is mightier than the sword* sweeps grandly, far more so than *talking beats fighting* or *Hey Joe, why not speak gently to Jim rather than attacking him?* Consider the lyrics of the rock song "Tumbling Dice." Are you moved by *"This low down bitchin' got my poor feet a itchin"?* Or do you think Mick Jagger should sing *"let's lose these annoying whiners?"*

Consider recreational sports and other play among friends. Deceptive tricks are innocent, fun, and accepted; friends steal signals and fake each other out. We're entertained by tall tales that everyone knows to be false, happily and agreeably so. Uncle Greg faux-rants about a faux-grievance; sister Emily teases her brother by exaggerating a minor problem. We ridicule issues that annoy or concern us, and lampoon people we care about. Honesty, accuracy, clarity, and transparency are hidden away so they won't ruin our fun or joy. Truth and transparency would deny our embarrassed need to cover up some sappy affection; it would block our teasing effort to vent some steam.

Imagination and Transcendence

Fiction entertains, while some falsehoods feed our highest aspirations:

> *Exaggeration, lies, bullshit, jokes, novels, metaphors, sarcasm... In each there is a clear sense in which we are not really presenting the truth, as we know it, based on the best available evidence. But... [while] some constitute morally objectionable behaviour, others are associated with art and poetry.*
>
> – Emar Maier

Myths and allegories, symbols and metaphor, allusions and analogies, and poetry are literary devices that *indirectly* pursue elusive unknowns. Among the most important of those unknowns is ultimate truth:

> *No one individual can look at truth – it blinds you. You look at it and you see one phase of it. Someone else looks at it and sees a*

slightly awry phase of it. But taken all together, the truth is in what they saw though nobody saw the truth intact.

– William Faulkner

Myths function in a vague middle ground between truth and fiction. They talk about things lacking evidence, weaving them into obviously imaginary stories. Metaphors, comparisons, analogies, and substitutions stand in for elusive truth(s). Literary techniques *allude* to those truths; they move us by their resonance with what we feel and believe, but cannot know. Though typically we think of myths as ancient false stories, they profoundly construct our mental frameworks, especially for vital things like births (creation), marriage, battles, and death. Myths *make coherent* the knowns and unknowns of our mental experience. [Keep in mind this idea of making things coherent: we'll see more about that in a few pages.]

Ancient poetry, scripture, and other forms of literature present many interpretive dilemmas, starting with the old writer's perspectives. To say that a person "walks on water" breaks what we know to be the laws of physics. It also defies the common sense of people in *any* historical age. Of course, the ancients were quite accustomed to mysterious events like epileptic fits (spirit possession?), visits from the dead in dreams (spirits again?), or seeing a newborn who stunningly resembles a dead ancestor (reincarnation?). Did the ancients really believe that people walk on water? Did someone actually *see* such a thing? Or did they *deceive themselves* into believing others had seen it? Isn't it more likely that the Biblical writer of Matthew used dreamlike language to express his reverence for a most extraordinary person? Maybe the writer's goal was not to declare a violation of natural laws, but rather to express a spiritual belief that a mysterious God transcends natural law. We can appreciate such poetry or theology for what probably is, rather than boxing it up as magical or superstitious thinking. The ancients may have been much more sophisticated than some of today's critics admit or even try to understand.

In case we're still feeling smug about how much we know that the ancients did not, consider again the outdated 'spirit theory of disease.' Long ago people believed that sick people are possessed by invisible spirits or ghosts. But isn't that strangely similar to our modern explanation that bodies are invaded by invisible bacteria and viruses? I never see with a naked eye those bacteria or viruses that I'm told are making me sick. But I believe the explanation, just as the ancients believed in unseen sickening spirits.

Poets and their critics know the special mental requirements for their art. The Scottish philosopher David Hume called poets *"liars by profession [who] always endeavor to give an air of truth to their fictions."* Plato wanted to ban poets from his perfect society. The English poet Coleridge realized that his own art required his readers to deceive themselves:

> *[My work must] procure for these shadows of imagination that willing suspension of disbelief for the moment, which constitutes poetic faith.* — Samuel Taylor Coleridge

A cyber illusionist observes:

> *When you give yourself over to art's deception, it becomes magic.*
> — Marco Tempest

Being literal about poetry, literature, and other arts strips them of their beauty. It impoverishes us. Poets help imaginative readers fly, leaving concrete thinkers grounded. Literalists might respond that poets think and speak like they're dreaming, even when they're awake. Whether we're poets or scientists, we deceive ourselves if we apply today's scientific standards to literally interpret art and literature, ancient or modern.

Ambition and Exploitation

Many deceptions simply are selfish efforts to gain something wanted or avoid something feared. We strive to be accepted, liked, or loved, and sometimes we accomplish that by telling people what they want to hear. A Fortune 150 CEO once described to me a handwritten card left for him in his new office by his predecessor:

> *Congratulations. You've now heard the truth for the very last time.*
> — Fortune 150 CEO

It's not that all CEOs are surrounded by scheming liars and suck-ups. It's that ambitious people want to please their bosses with good performance. Their strong wish to give good news limits their ability to spot problems. With "blind ambition" they deceive themselves first, then the boss. What's the solution? Hire information gatherers whose job is to listen skeptically throughout the organization, and to get the real scoop from people near the customers. Formally authorized skeptics don't have a vested interest in saying what the boss wants to hear. They don't need his cherished plans to succeed brilliantly, as others are hoping (and convincing each other).

When bad news can't be hidden and we want to avoid loss or blame, our explanations and excuses can get creative. Highly intelligent or creative people are even more able to produce self-serving rationalizations. Rather than accepting bad news or challenging a too-favorable report, they create an interpretation (a silver lining?) that delivers what they want to hear.

After we've deceived someone – and even after regretting it – we may deceive *again* with persuasive cover-ups. President Richard Nixon's White House Counsel, John Dean, described the Watergate scandal of the 1970s in just such terms. It began with little evasions and minor deceptions, then grew by degrees. Somewhere in a grey area the perpetrators crossed over into outright lies, the famed "coverup." Lies led to potential criminal acts.

After a period of scandal led to a presidential resignation, Nixon's successor Gerald Ford proposed an extremely simple antidote:

I believe that truth is the glue that holds government together, not only our Government, but civilization itself. That bond, though strained, is unbroken at home and abroad. In all my public and private acts as your President, I expect to follow my instincts of openness and candor with full confidence that honesty is always the best policy in the end. My fellow Americans, our long national nightmare is over.

> – Gerald Ford, remarks upon being sworn in as President, 1974

We all know what it's like to try avoiding detection, embarrassment, or punishment for the mistakes we'd like to hide. Compared to Watergate, our coverups are different in degree. But they're not different in kind.

Political life is full of incentives to claim that a policy works grandly. Sometimes it's like putting lipstick on a pig. Advocates declare that an opponent's policy has utterly failed, like a mirage in the barren desert. Hype draws exaggerated cartoons of the normal ups and downs, strengths and weaknesses, in any human effort. Sometimes we totalize, expanding a single incident into a broad conclusion. For example, we expand *I failed* into *I'm a failure*; *you offended Ted* becomes *you're offensive.*

Natural rivalries can grow into unhealthy bitterness and cynicism, as satirized by an Irish playwright:

It's not enough that I should succeed, others should fail.

> – Oscar Wilde

Uncountable numbers of people want something from you and me, to benefit them. Giving up that something (like our money) *may* also be in our

142

interest. It can lead to a productive exchange, like buying a home. That's a healthy market economy! But skillful promoters use tricks of the trade to convince us to buy what we don't need, or too much of what we do need. Partisans and advocates work to persuade us that their cause should be ours. Today's victimhood culture leads people to avoid responsibility for disappointing outcomes, blaming misfortunes on people they've never met.

British broadcaster Alexis Conran has illustrated these techniques with a reality TV team that fools passersby in some way. Conran then stops and explains to the targets how the deceptions had worked. The techniques always involve the cooperation of the victims, who were persuaded to suppress their better judgment.

> *We set aside our better judgment all the time... the real work of persuasion takes place inside our heads... and it's up to us to realize when we're being taken. In truth, no one is out there offering us something for nothing. Whether it's our money, our data or our time [and attention], we're always giving back something in return.*
>
> – Alexis Conran

Conran identifies five key tactics of con men:
- **misdirection** (or distraction, a favorite of magicians)
- **urgency** (we make more mistakes under pressure)
- **social compliance** (submitting to perceived expertise, authority)
- **social proof** (i.e., the bandwagon effect) and
- **opportunity** (when a buyer is naïve or un-skeptical)

Our greed for bargains underlies a seller's big "opportunity." Fear of missing out (FOMO) plays a part in our attraction to bandwagons.

It's been said, with obvious hype, that 1% of people casually lie (or cheat, or steal); 1% would never do so; and the rest of us are honest *if the conditions are right.* Consider a situation that's doubly tempting: the job interview. Both parties may see the other as a solution for their needs. Each is motivated to believe dubious claims. According to Robert Feldman, a professor of psychological and brain sciences, *"It's a situation almost designed to encourage lying."* Feldman's research indicates that job candidates tell, on average, 2-3 lies in a 10-15 minute interview.

Prof. Dan Ariely's research has identified factors that raise or lower our temptation to shave the truth a bit... to take a little advantage, just this once or twice. We're more tempted to lie if:

- we've lied before
- others seem to be lying
- we can rationalize deceit

- our culture permits lying
- a lie may help someone else
- we're exhausted & undisciplined

On the other hand, we can prevent or diminish lying by:

- supervision
- attaching a signature
- receiving regular moral reminders and reinforcements
  (e.g., from religious activities, parents, family, or friends)

- having made an honor pledge/oath

Advocacy and Partisanship

Partisans are known for enthusiastic exaggeration if not propaganda. After a recent election, I read a blog to get more insight into what a friend described as "how I feel that's described in a way I can't express on my own." Candidate Trump was described, among many insults, as a bigot and racist; his supporters therefore also must be bigots and racists. Trump's supporters responded in kind, declaring (just as mistakenly) that supporters of a "socialist" candidate must also be socialists. One respondent called out a self-deceived critic, who seemed to think that name-calling would change the minds of his opponents. The respondent wrote: "that's alright, just keep berating us and maybe we'll come around someday."

When dealing with adversaries, it's common to be sly, to use guile and skillful ambiguity. These tactics are common when dealing with people we can't trust, or who have conflicting goals. Skillful politicians are masters of ambiguity: they serve divided, diverse populations by mastering the art of evasion (if not deception). This frustrates opponents. But most importantly, it enables supporters to believe *what they wish to be true*:

> *When you want to help people, you tell them the truth. When you want to help yourself, you tell them what they want to hear.... A talented con man, or a slick politician, does not waste his time trying to convince knowledgeable skeptics. His job is to keep the true believers believing. He is not going to convince the others anyway. ... The fact that so many successful politicians are such shameless liars is not only a reflection on them, it is also a reflection on us. When the people want the impossible, only liars can satisfy.*
>
> – Thomas Sowell

To get support from diverse voters, politicians circulate messages that hearers can mold to their own needs. Said more plainly: candidates almost always tell voters what they want to hear. Political speeches or advertisements typically feature evasions, if not outright fantasies or deceptions. One favorite tactic is to embrace whatever principle produces today's desired outcome. The principle can later be switched when tomorrow's desired outcomes require it. According to one astute observer:

> *[In politics], all process arguments are insincere.*
>
> –Michael Barone

A journalist puts it bluntly:

> *[It's an] iron principle that the partisan version of everything is almost always a lie.*   – Holman Jenkins, Jr.

Partisans commonly pretend that their cause is based on principle rather than power. They may even believe it themselves. Majority legislators hate the filibuster: it frustrates their agenda, so they complain it denies the will of the democratic majority. But when the same party becomes the minority, the filibuster is suddenly a pillar of minority rights, an essential check and balance against tyranny of the majority. Race discrimination is an outrage, except when affirmative action produces different racial outcomes. Minority rights are essential, until small states – a population minority – deny the will of the majority (i.e. the populous states) in the Electoral College. [This odd Constitutional mechanism was established specifically to protect small states from being dominated by larger ones. In short, America's founders didn't want big cities to tilt the whole country toward urban interests. Guess which interests now hate the Electoral College!]

We demand inclusivity and equality for everyone, then require that special oppressed communities have separate accommodations on campuses. We demand equality before the law, then tack on special penalties for thought crimes -- as if an oppressed criminal is less guilty, or a privileged victim is less dead. On most such issues there can be good reasons for differential or equal treatment, but we shouldn't pretend that one conclusion is righteous and the other is an abomination. We've seen that principles can be applied inconsistently, often for good reason. But in some cases that "reason" turns out to be power, ideology, and/or self-interest.

There's also a problem of knowing what politicians are actually saying about these kinds of problem (if they're saying anything at all). One political journalist says that politics is cynicism cloaked in ritualized hypocrisy. The results are then delivered to us by media figures whose impartiality has bowed to ideology, mission, or purpose. So we get media filtering behavior that looks a lot like that universal human quirk – motivated reasoning – including double standards:

A problem of late has been a national media that, in key instances, has preferred to protect the lies and sins of its favorites while exaggerating and even inventing those of politicians it opposes.

– Holman Jenkins, Jr.

Deception in politics has been observed for thousands of years, at least since ancient Rome:

Be lavish in your promises. The masses would much rather follow a false prophet, than countenance a flat refusal.   – Cicero

A chameleon on plaid.

– Herbert Hoover, describing Franklin Roosevelt

Perot has been dubbed the "Rorschach candidate," which permits such widely divergent followers to gather under his leadership mantle, projecting onto his "substance-free" ambiguity what they wish to see.   – Jerrold Post, Chicago Tribune

Government officials — whoever resides in the White House — are professional liars. They lie haughtily in the interest of 'national security,' sheepishly in the interest of saving face, and passionately when their jobs are on the line.   – Sam Adler Bell

Lest we be too harsh on politicians, let's remember that voters *demand* what we want to hear. Candidates who scold their voters are losing candidates. And how can a candidate know better than a voter what's in her best interest? After pointing a finger at deceiving politicians, let's look in the mirror. Do we really expect them to tell us unpleasant and unflattering truths, or is pandering more likely? We can expect chatbots and similar technologies to be highly skilled at learning what we want to hear, and especially capable of using our rampant confirmation bias to deceive us.

147

People tend to bend the truth to avoid conflict or embarrassment. When we stick to remarks about the bright side, others more easily like us (or at least the guarded persona we present to the world):

> *Most people follow a script... because they're afraid that if they say what they really feel, people won't like them. And they'd rather be liked than be honest... I decided that my truth-telling had caused enough destruction, that it was no longer worth it. There must be things others knew that I didn't, I thought, reasons why dishonesty made others genuinely happy... I started with small talk. I asked the same safe questions the people around me asked and pretended to be satisfied with vague or avoidant answers. I tried to remind myself that this people-pleasing was normal, that it was what everyone wanted from me. I tried to find pleasure in being liked, having jobs and friendships and romances. But all along, my honest brain kept telling me that I had become a con artist... These days, I try to save my honesty for those who want it. And when someone won't be honest with me, I can understand why. I still hope people will give me the unvarnished truth. But sometimes we have to start with the script to build enough trust to throw [the script] away.*
>
> *– Michael Leviton*

***

So how can we ever find political agreement amid so much diversity, conflict, and evasion? According to an astute observer of psychological and social matters, persuasion *never* results from a hostile takedown:

> *No one has ever been insulted into agreement. We need opposing viewpoints to challenge our own. If we're wrong, the best way to learn it is through challenges from our friends on the other side of the issue.*
>
> *– Arthur Brooks*

148

Friends – not enemies – are more likely to persuade. Focusing solely on the merits of our own thinking builds up our own blinders and ignorance. In 1859 the British philosopher John Stuart Mill brilliantly described people who get lost in arguments for their own causes:

> *He who knows only his own side of the case knows little of that. His reasons may be good, and no one may have been able to refute them. But if he is equally unable to refute the reasons on the opposite side, if he does not so much as know what they are, he has no ground for preferring either opinion... Nor is it enough that he should hear the opinions of adversaries from his own teachers, presented as they state them, and accompanied by what they offer as refutations. He must be able to hear them from persons who actually believe them...he must know them in their most plausible and persuasive form.*   – John Stuart Mill

Mill recommends that we genuinely try to understand opposing views. This naturally *excludes* our tendency to exaggerate opposing views, turning them into scarecrows or 'straw men' that we then can then confidently knock down.

Here's our test: would an opponent *accept and use our characterization* of what (s)he believes?

Nature and Warfare

For anyone who may still think intentional deception is *essentially* bad, to be avoided almost always, we may ask: Would you deny deceptive powers to prey animals, whose lives are constantly at stake?

[An] arms race between deception and detection is common in nature.

– Pascal Boyer

Animals, including some humans, struggle to survive in a natural world that's "red in tooth and claw." Transparency in nature can be a death trap. So can physical weakness, or a low capacity for shrewdness and guile.

In civilization, enemy combatants are the equivalent of natural predators. They're committed to destroying us, or at least the things we hold dear. Deception is rampant and easily justified in literal human warfare, where thousands or millions of lives may be at stake.

All warfare is deception. – Sun Tzu

One tool of deceptive persuasion is propaganda, which denies an enemy's very humanity. Editorial cartoons depict enemies as bears, snakes, rats and more; it's far easier to kill a predator or rodent than another human. Studies have indicated that long after a war is over, children's cartoons signify villainous characters by having them speak with foreign accents. An example is Natasha Badenov's Russian flair in the *Rocky and Bullwinkle Show*, on American TV during the 1960s Cold War. Such tribal signals communicate subliminally that "foreign is suspicious." Is it deceptive – is it lying – to convey subliminal messages to be subconsciously consumed?

Lines between friend or foe can be elusive, yet even clear lines fade as circumstances change. Allies can become belligerents (and vice versa) within a few short years. Japanese and German enemies became American allies a few years after World War II. Soviet allies morphed to Cold War

150

enemies virtually overnight (historically speaking). Individuals can shift allegiance even faster: lovers become combatants within minutes, then reunite within hours. According to studies, *hostile* business mediators resolve more disputes than do polite ones; adversaries unite to face a common enemy. Police called to a domestic disturbance sometimes face a suddenly united couple who see a common opponent at their door. As the saying has it, all's fair in love or war. Who is justified in deceiving whom? And is deception really the best way to get good outcomes?

Civilized norms, like social cooperation and the rule of law, must be well developed if moral virtues are to displace nature's violent, predatory forces. Even so, violence and exploitation are never fully extinguished; they're merely repressed. The best possible outcome is to minimize the causes and benefits of uncivil behavior, perhaps to dampen if not minimize beastly acts.

Some cultures, especially ancient ones, permit or encourage lying to outsiders. For much of history, all foreigners were assumed to be adversaries. Modern behavior is still tribal in some respects, even as we aspire to ever more universal standards of morality.

Tribal mindsets emphasize *difference* and are suspicious of it. This mindset lacks the trust and cooperation that might convert opponents into friends. President Abraham Lincoln faced exactly this enormous challenge in reconciling North and South after the U.S. Civil War, and he doubled down on the value of friendship:

Why, madam, do I not destroy my enemies when I make them my friends?
                                                        – Abraham Lincoln

Trust and Confidence

Even undetected lies are corrosive. They cause incoherence, then cover-ups. Telling lies eventually diminishes self-respect. Each lie lowers the barrier to the next lie. Consider my friend who had an extra-marital affair, and later said about his wife: *"she didn't know, but I did – and when I looked in the mirror, I saw a liar."*

Teams cannot be efficient if members withhold or distort information. Lying dilutes our capacity to solve problems accurately, to achieve justice, or to improve collaboration and competition. Yet lying also can provide an escape from facing problems head on:

> *Harsh truths violate social norms, and so people avoid telling them.... Most people lie around two to four times per day... What's more, the habit of telling lies, even little ones, is contagious. It doesn't take long for a habit to become a norm, and a norm to become a culture.* — Professor Tessa West

Among the greatest negative effects of lying may be the loss of **trust and confidence**, which have been built slowly, in small increments, accumulating over a long time. This slow building pattern describes how we grow wealth; it describes how civilization itself is developed. Betrayal abruptly damages trust in the same way that folly can quickly diminish prosperity and civilized collaboration. War degrades it all.

> *Civilization is an intricate and precarious web of human relationships, laboriously built and readily destroyed.* — Will and Ariel Durant

Trust also can be eroded in barely perceptible steps over time, which raises doubts, suspicions, uncertainty, delays and security costs as victims build defenses against more loss. Eroded trust destroys community at many

152

levels, reminding us that truth and trustworthiness are key pillars of human connection.

Rebuilding confidence or trust is slow, hard, uncertain, exhausting – and wonderful when it succeeds. Yet rebuilding can lead to abandonment if some wounds are too deep to heal. Then we must forfeit *the illusion* – the *false hope* – that wholeness could be restored with a lover or a friend.

Consider a surveillance state that once paid citizens to betray acts of resistance among friends and family. When such betrayals are eventually recognized, citizens become ever more wary: *who else is spying on me?* Every relationship becomes infected with suspicion. This is the legacy of the Stasi, a domestic spy agency in the former East Germany (the GDR). A reunified Germany has given the public access to Stasi files to expose the GDR's abuse of allegiance to the regime:

> *The destruction of trust was one of the most painful legacies of their experiences in the GDR. The dense informer network meant that everyone spied on one another. Many did not find out who had informed on them until decades later, when they requested their Stasi file. One woman... was devastated [to discover] that the man she loved was informing on her. Still reeling from this betrayal, she later found out another close friend was also spying on her. A man... recounted how his intention to leave the country was betrayed, and so instead of getting out, he was thrown in jail. Ten years later, on receiving his Stasi file, he found out that the person who betrayed him was his girlfriend. "I trust only a few people I have known a long time," Hendschke told me. "I only get to know new people with a certain distance. My life today is pretty isolated."*
>
> – Charlotte Bailey, Atlantic magazine

People with guilty minds can seek relief responsibly through apology or confession. Others "forget" their violations or errors, pretending they never happened. Some "liars" are so desensitized or rationalized in their transgressions – a pattern common in addicts – that they're barely aware of their deceptions. Just like their trusting and gullible hearers, many liars remain in the dark, but probably not forever:

> *You can fool all the people some of the time and some of the people all the time, but you cannot fool all the people all the time.*
>
> – Abraham Lincoln
>
> *Fool me once, shame on you. Fool me twice, shame on me.*
>
> – Italian proverb
>
> *At the length truth will out.*
>
> – Shakespeare, in Merchant of Venice

We've seen that people might honorably lie to *prevent* harm or suffering. Now we see that some lie to *inflict* harm or suffering to "serve a greater cause," such as loyalty to authority. Tyrants have been credited with saying *"you can't make an omelet without breaking eggs"* – a colorful way to say *the ends justify the violent means*. Much boils down to whether that higher and nobler cause is morally justified – producing more good than evil.

> *Mass murderers and serial killers typically have reasons for why they commit horrible crimes, but they do not have good reasons. It's only when people have morally good reasons that we excuse or condone their behavior.*   – Internet Encyclopedia of Philosophy

What are truths?

With these examples as background, let's dig a bit deeper.

A great challenge of the modern age is our complicated and conflicted understanding of truth(s). Diverse people certainly have diverse *understandings* of truth; this encourages the widely held view that truths themselves are diverse, contextual, and particular. Such truths are spelled with a small t, rather than the capital T of universal, objective Truth.

But not so long ago it was commonly believed that Truth is independent of perception or context... and that such objective Truth might be discoverable by science. Long before that, Truth was commonly thought to be revealed by religion and spiritual practices, though imperfectly and only in part. In ancient India, the partial and mistaken perception of a greater Truth was illustrated by a parable of the blind man and the elephant:

> *Blind men heard [of] a strange animal, called an elephant... none of them were aware of its shape and form. They said: "We must inspect and know it by touch... the first person, whose hand landed on the trunk, said "This being is like a thick snake." For one whose hand reached its ear, it seemed like a kind of fan. Another person, whose hand was upon its leg, said the elephant is a pillar like a tree-trunk. The blind man with his hand upon its side said the elephant "is a wall". Another who felt its tail, described it as a rope. The last felt its tusk, stating the elephant is hard, smooth, and like a spear.*
>
> – Indian Parable of the Elephant

The Christian Apostle Paul expressed his experience of fragmented truth, including his hope to one day see ultimate Truth. His words are beautifully rendered in English by the 1611 King James translation of the Bible:

> *For now we see through a glass, darkly; but then face to face: now I know* in *part; but then shall I know even as also I am known.*
>
> – 1 Corinthians 13:12, KJV (1611)

In today's less poetic but clearer language:

155

Now we see things imperfectly, like puzzling reflections in a mirror, but then we will see everything with perfect clarity. All that I know now is partial and incomplete, but then I will know everything completely, just as God now knows me completely.

– New Living translations, 1996-2007

Even as late as the mid-1600s, the great French mathematician and physicist Blaise Pascal said we know truth not only by reason, but also by feeling:

The heart has its reasons which reason knows nothing of...
We know the truth not only by the reason, but by the heart.

– Blaise Pascal

Charles Peirce, an American logician and scientist of the early 20th century, agreed that after we manage to find some access to truth, we understand it only imperfectly. Peirce added that *some truths are truer than others,* and real truths gain acceptance over time. So "the truth" is in a unanimously agreed opinion that's "fated" to occur through our investigations.

The opinion which is fated to be ultimately agreed to by all who investigate, is what we mean by the truth, and the object represented in this opinion is the real.   – Charles Peirce

On this reckoning, true and false are *not* binary values. They exist on a sliding scale, a continuum, a slippery slope. Absolute Truth may thus be at the end of a kind of rainbow, a spectrum of partial-truths. Here **truths (and Truth) are a complicated mixture of abstract considerations** including context, uncertainty, and what precisely we mean when we speak of "truth."

Typically in the sciences, truth is *more* binary. Sand is not nutritious, whatever someone believes. But in poetry, literature, and scripture many "true" interpretations bring richness rather than error. There's no end to subjective disputes about elusive truths, so we fight over what the "science" says, desperate for an objective anchor to support *our* subjective views. If that fails, rather than change our opinions we seek other anchors (principles, or logic, or arguments, etc.) to affirm our beliefs. We resist any allegation that our beliefs are deficient and should change.

Some statements are <u>neither true nor false</u>, like declarations about the future ("*Smith will win the election... The Giants will defeat the Cowboys... Everything's going to be all right... The earth will be destroyed.*") This category includes not only predictions, but also visions (a.k.a. "prophecies" in ancient times). Visions express a coherent view of what can or should be. Speculations cannot meet a standard of proof; they're *not yet* true or false. Of course, some predictions are more reliably based on historical data, precedents, or principles, such as physical laws. But even such well-supported predictions are not "true" until they become facts. We risk fooling ourselves when we're too confident about our truths, especially predictive or hypothetical ones. Consider this example from a 2022 radio broadcast:

> *If Ukraine had nuclear weapons, Russia would not have invaded Ukraine. That's just a simple fact.*   – David Marples, historian

This "simple fact" doesn't correspond to any reality: Ukraine did NOT have nuclear weapons when Russia invaded. Yet "would not have" is a clear signal that the observer is speculating; he's delivering a convincing opinion, not a fact. This is a "coherent" speculative statement (more on that later!) saying that Russia *surely wouldn't* risk invading a nuclear-armed Ukraine.

As much more "news" coverage goes beyond facts to analyze and interpret "what it means," facts become more mixed with opinions or speculations. Sorting this out requires deliberate, keenly critical attention, often in debate. As a rule of thumb, remember this: predicted events are literally unreal – they are imaginary – and are not yet true until the moment they occur.

There's a special class of statements that are <u>both true and false</u>. Consider the self-referencing sentence *This statement is false.* If the sentence is true, then it's false (and vice versa). Self-referencing logic challenges mathematicians and computer designers, but it's rare and causes few problems for most of us.

Finally, serious problems <u>do</u> arise in the vast number of claims that are true in *some sense* but not in others – or true in *some situations* but not in others. These half-truths may well outnumber truths and lies combined. Far too often we simplify and totalize them into full truths.

> *Partial truths or half-truths are more insidious than total falsehoods. [Falsehoods can be refuted with one exception to their claims, but] a partial truth is plausible because some evidence does support it, and it is easy to assume that it is the total truth. [Two accurate ways of describing someone's identity] are not mistaken identities; they are partial identities [among many other identities]. Neither one nor both is the whole truth.*
> – Samuel P. Huntington, *Who Are We?*

Disagreements about ambiguity are a big source of accusations about lying. Disputes are fueled by differences in how an idea is applied, incomplete information, or subtle differences in definition. If we accept that most truths and beliefs are contextual rather than universal, then there's even greater scope for imprecise words, discordant interpretations, and incompatible applications. All can be misunderstood as intentional deceptions.

Ambiguous truth is a troublesome but important aspect of law enforcement. It's simply very hard to prove someone's intent, motivation, or awareness. This is one of the reasons that the law penalizes only certain types of lying. The constitutional guarantee of *freedom of speech* is so broadly stated that it includes the freedom to speak falsehoods. Of course this freedom is being vigorously challenged by people who think they speak the truth, that others do not, and that police must suppress false speech from the other guys.

Courts have held that even *statements known by a speaker to be literally false* are covered by first amendment protections. Permitted speech includes satire, parody, and hyperbole – all literally false, yet effective in expressing political opposition. Penalizing them verges on policing thought and speech. Courts have held that free speech does *not* protect fighting words, true threats, defamation, or incitement. Nuances and ambiguities of this issue are at the heart of controversies about hateful or false speech.

To complicate this further, the subtleties of free speech laws differ by country. In Great Britain a writer can be prosecuted for libel or slander while the same case may not succeed under more permissive U.S. law.

Fraud – *theft by deception* – is a crime nearly everywhere. But *theft* is what causes trouble, not the deception. A seller who wants repeat customers soon learns that deceiving them loses their repeat purchases. One-time transactions are most vulnerable to deceptive practices. To this the law says *caveat emptor: buyer beware*. Teasing out truth in deceptive remarks is a job for a skeptical listener, not the police. What deceives me may not deceive more-experienced you. Truth spoken may not be truth heard.

A conviction for perjury requires lying *under oath* in a judicial proceeding. By contrast, lies to friends, bosses, spouses, the media etc. generally cannot be prosecuted. A lying lion on Twitter or TV often becomes a lamb under oath, suddenly unable to remember incriminating details. Savvy lawyers know that a weak memory cannot be prosecuted, so hazy "recollections" offer a refuge for liars. Certain special cases, such as a material lie to a federal investigator or employee, can indeed be prosecuted. For those of us lacking power to prosecute people who lie to us, a rule of thumb is simply to be wary, especially among people you don't yet trust. *Listener* beware. Remember also that wishful thinking abounds: we especially and always must be on guard against self-deception. *Self* beware.

Correspondence or Coherence

Here we're briefly entering some deeper waters. Hopefully, I've earned enough of your trust that you'll bear with me for a few pages that are more deeply probing. I believe you'll find the payoff to be enormous.

Truth can be understood in at least two ways: as *correspondence to reality* or *coherence within a bigger picture.*

- Science and reason have objective standards for truth that *corresponds* to observable, measurable reality. These standards are independent of stories and individual minds. They align with a materialistic point of view because physical things can be observed and measured by objective techniques.

- Religion and the arts pursue truths that *cohere* within the mind and imagination. Coherent truths emphasize subjective and metaphysical dimensions – ideals, meaning, identity, purpose, destiny, etc. Spiritual or literary frames of reference tilt toward coherence rather than correspondence, but so do the views of some mathematicians and rationalists. Standards for what is coherent in the imagination are notoriously personalized, slippery, and immeasurable, while rational coherence depends on the rules and discipline of logic.

Correspondence to fact begins with evidence – observed details. *Inductive* (bottom-up) reasoning then builds those details into a general theory, principle, or "law." The philosopher-scientist Aristotle emphasized this approach, known as *empiricism*, begins with collecting data. Some 1500 years later, the theologian St. Thomas Aquinas revived Aristotelian thought, including his view that truth is correspondence with reality:

Truth is the equation of thought and thing. – St. Thomas Aquinas

Eight centuries later, a 20th century British mathematician and logician echoed both Aristotle and Aquinas:

Truth consists in some form of correspondence between belief and fact.
– Bertrand Russell

This is what most of us understand when we speak of truth; it's what we've been taught in science courses. Less well taught is that all conclusions based on observations can be disproven or superseded with new data; skepticism or doubt are thus vital aspects of empirical science. Everything we know is tentative, subject to change from new and better observations. We can push this a bit further by saying that accepted theories derive their power from rigorous logical rules AND from the agreement of skilled, well-informed observers on how to apply those rules. Sometimes science produces rival interpretations, such as whether light is a wave or particle.

The understanding of truth as coherence proceeds in the opposite order from inductive (bottom-up) observation or reasoning. *Deductive (top down) reasoning* begins with universal truths and deduces (*derives*) conclusions. It proceeds from a general, overarching concept to describe specific, imperfect examples of that concept.

> *[T]o say that a statement is true or false is to say that it coheres or*
> *fails to cohere with a system of other statements; that it is a member*
> *of a system whose elements are related to each other by ties of logical*
> *implication, as the elements in a system of pure mathematics are*
> *related.*   – Alan R. White

Some of history's greatest mathematicians and intellectual system-builders – like Baruch Spinoza, Gottfried Leibniz, and G.W.F. Hegel – developed what are called <u>coherentist</u> accounts of truth. Their coherence is grounded in *logic and reason*. But coherence also may be grounded in *intuitive judgments*. Recall the utterly simple words used by Egyptian thinker

Hypatia: "truth is opinion." This means truth relies not in a correspondence with reality, but rather in what we judge to be *coherent* and believable:

Truth is a point of view, and so is changeable. – Hypatia of Alexandria

The Greek philosopher Plato is known for his concept of "forms." He said any particular table is a momentary portrayal – a "shadow" – of the pure, ideal essence of "table-ness." There are many tables but only one form of a table. Ditto for beds, chairs, and all material things for which humans use conceptual categories. Plato says we live in a world of shadows – projected images of pure, coherent, perfect forms – that we access through Reason.

Deriving specifics from an ultimate, general principle appeals powerfully to our emotional need for stability and certainty. It relates to an intuition about abstract ideals – to the gratifying, even awed feeling we get from contemplating a perfect "form" or concept (like Truth, Beauty, the Good, and God). Ultimate, infinite forms suggest hierarchical categories in which particular examples reflect that general, absolute form. Deducing specific examples from abstract general forms was a major feature of ancient and medieval thought. Such thinking suggests that we better understand specific earthly examples by understanding more about their perfect forms, which may even relate to an ultimate kind of meaning or purpose.

Of course, such hierarchical thinking is vigorously disputed, even despised, by those who see nature's processes (like evolution) as random and arbitrary. It's no wonder that these debates can get, shall we say, testy.

For millions if not billions of people, existence makes sense – it is coherent – *only* if we believe in the existence of infinite absolutes like God, Truth, Beauty, and Goodness. Science can't confirm or refute metaphysical things (those things beyond physical reality) because we can't observe them. But people can and do *believe* or *reason* that non-physical things are necessary to our spiritual and moral existence. Absolutes are seen as logically necessary, or at least overwhelmingly implied beyond reasonable doubt.

The medieval scholar St. Thomas Aquinas said that *analogy* is another way to think about these things. He said we can know about ultimate things by comparison with worldly and real things (for example, as creatures reflect something about their creator). We also might think of absolutes as the endpoints of an *infinite progression* from good to better to best (or true to truer to Truth). This echoes the idea of an *infinite regression* of causes, back to a first cause or to creation.

So debate never ceases about things we've never seen, heard, smelled, or touched. Yet intuitively we perceive them.

Our beliefs about absolutes (and about "ultimate concerns," as theologian Paul Tillich put it) turn out to be highly resistant to proof or refutation. A Platonic "perfect form" surely is coherent; our supposedly coherent beliefs about them fit into a whole system of other things we believe to be true. Losing one belief could threaten the others, so we're motivated to defend our belief systems vigorously. We're also quite motivated to deceive ourselves about how reliable and foolproof our beliefs are.

Quantum physics has shown recently that truth may *include contradiction.* To say this another way, one reality can be seen from multiple perspectives, each coherent but contradicting others:

> *Viewed from multiple perspectives, a single object may be perceived as having inconsistent, even contradictory, properties. It is an important – and mathematically validated – principle of quantum mechanics, [Physicist and Nobel recipient Frank] Wilczek believes that the principle can be applied to other domains].*

> – Christopher Levenick

Applying this idea to "multiple domains" quickly gets to the issues of diversity and "versions" of truth. It brings yet more challenges to the idea of unitary, absolute, or coherent Truth. A twentieth-century novelist recounts an experience that shaped her view of how elusive truth can be:

> *Going to law courts is a good education for a novelist. It provides you with the most extravagant material, and it teaches the near impossibility of reaching the truth.*   – Sybille Bedford

I'm told that a recently retiring U.S. federal judge left the bench in part because "expert" witnesses so often testify to truths that contradict the testimony of other "experts." Such "truths" may be chosen, not proven.

Most of us claim that we want facts and objective truth, but our behavior indicates otherwise. Even scientists and other experts prefer coherent beliefs that support *what we prefer to be true*. Prioritizing *our* perspectives against conflicting opinions is a key feature of motivated reasoning. Remember, motivated reasoning chooses or rejects "facts" based on whether they fit a favored concept, theory, or narrative. To curb this universal human tendency, good scientists cultivate a habit of skepticism. Anyone – scientists or others – cannot be trusted to be impartial if they've already committed to a belief about the issue at hand. Ideologies are especially corrupting in this way: an ideological scientist or judge is a walking contradiction.

It's easy to see the connection here with motivated journalism, which brings us so much advocacy that in turn leads directly to claims about "fake news." Convictions are key drivers of factional politics, religious conflict, political uses of science, and dueling versions of nearly everything.

It's worth checking every now and again whether our convictions need a tune-up in this ever-changing world.

Theories are Stories

In an important sense, *scientific theories are themselves stories*: they bind lonely facts into greater explanations and truths. Even a scientific hypothesis –a testable guess – is a "story" that's proposed as a first step toward validated scientific truth. So we argue over competing stories or "narratives" to make sense of it all. Conflicting stories are featured in science and literature, politics, religion, sports, and even within one person's turbulent introspection. The following quotes from a social theorist, a judge, a novelist, and a popular composer show their very similar views on the vitally important role of stories in seeking truth:

Man is in his actions and practice, as well as in his fictions, essentially a story-telling animal.... I can only answer the question "What am I to do?" if I can answer the prior question "Of what story or stories do I find myself a part?" – Alasdair MacIntyre, philosopher

The life of the law has not been logic: it has been experience... the law embodies the story of a nation's development through many centuries, and it cannot be dealt with as if it contained only the axioms and corollaries of a book of mathematics.
                    – Oliver Wendell Holmes, Supreme Court Justice

Man is the Storytelling Animal... in stories are his identity, his meaning, and his lifeblood.   – Salman Rushdie, novelist

My songs were always expressing very internal thoughts in music, and you hope that these things which mean something to you will resonate with other people. We go shopping in the popular culture for our own mythology and our tribe. We assemble things to speak for us.   – James Taylor, composer

So how do we judge which stories are true? Must every true story correspond strictly to *one* objective reality? Might it correspond to only one of many realities? Can truth be found in a coherent fictional story that does not correspond to any observable facts of the material world?

Philosopher of science Karl Popper gained a substantial reputation for showing how scientific conclusions are *always tentative*. He said scientific statements must be *falsifiable*. Observational reasoning can never be exhaustive because it's impossible to observe all instances past *and future*. We see only through the windows available to us; those windows include our particular human senses (and their limitations), as well as our point of view and context (and their limitations). So empirical laws are never ultimate or final; they're always subject to refutation and improvement.

In so far as a scientific statement speaks about reality, it must be falsifiable; and in so far as it is not falsifiable, it does not speak about reality.   – Karl Popper

Scientific advances typically are based on

- *new observations (*as with Pasteur's discovery of germs, or Galileo's observations of a falling ball and feather) or
- *new theories* that better explain old observations (as in the Copernican shift to a sun-centered universe, or Kepler's discovery of the mathematical laws of planetary motion).

Newton's laws of motion, published in 1687, accurately forecasted movements at the speeds and scales of everyday life, as seen by the unaided human eye. But Newton's laws turned out to be wholly inadequate for describing celestial motion at the speed of light, or particle movement at a subatomic scale. Since Newton, scientists have observed that the properties of physics are quite different at a cosmological scale (where gravity is described as curvatures in space) and at nano scale (e.g. gold metal doesn't

166

have a gold color). Newton's laws were not "wrong" for their time and place; they simply applied to a limited span of space and time. They still do. But now, with newer tools like advanced telescopes and microscopes, we can observe the universe at those higher and lower scales, and we've developed new laws of physics. These laws go far beyond Newtonian mechanics to describe what we're seeing with better optical technology.

For each of us, applying Popper's falsifiability principle leads us to ask: *what specific new information would change my opinion or conclusion*? Are my beliefs falsifiable, based on fact – or are they impermeable articles of faith, like a religious belief? This test is a superb cure for arrogance and overweening certainty. It cuts deeply into our comfortable love affair with self-serving conviction, and with the motivated reasoning that defends it.

Anyone, on most any day, can see that the sun moves across our sky from east to west… except it doesn't. It merely *appears* to do so from our limited perspective. For centuries now students have learned that Polish polymath Mikołaj Kopernik (Copernicus in Latin) revolutionized cosmology in 1543, explaining that Earth moves around the sun, not the sun around the Earth. As scientists say, our solar system is heliocentric, not geocentric. For half a millennium, we've well understood that *humans are not at the center of the universe*, yet it remains common to say the sun rises in our east and sets in our west. This 'untrue' view still works well within our daily frame of perception. Similarly, ballplayers have a working knowledge of how to pick up resting balls and throw them, even though Kepler's Laws have described motion otherwise. (Kepler showed that objects move continually unless interrupted by forces like gravity or contact with other objects). Photos from space now show us that rainbows are actually half of a colorful circle. Optical laws, unusual angles of light, and limited perspectives combine to create a beautiful semicircular appearance that's cut off at our visual horizon. With rainbows we see only about half of a fully circular truth.

Habits of perception and analysis die hard. They last indefinitely *after* we know they're wrong or incomplete. A workable falsehood is a solution or belief that's *good enough*: "almost" works well enough in most situations, far beyond 'hand grenades and horseshoes.' As finance professionals say:

The perfect is the enemy of the good. – Wall Street proverb

It should be no wonder that persuading others usually requires much more than spotting a logical contradiction, or telling a more coherent story.

People defend their beliefs for good reason: they perceive them to be workable, productive, and "true." Typically we replace our beliefs only when they fail our needs AND friends warmly lead us to see a better way. Opponents or critics rarely compel change, even to a clearly better alternative. Change is better promoted when we *remove obstacles* to it; it's best if others can see change as their own idea. In other words: people are loved, encouraged, and welcomed into lasting change, not beaten into it.

Truth is Tentative, Incomplete, Partial

Whether they correspond or cohere, *all* truths are tentative. Said more plainly, our truth(s) is or are often wrong. Even "right" truths can be improved in scope, detail, clarity, and effective application. Karl Popper specified that scientific truth is falsifiable, but religious or poetic truths also are subject to change and improvement. An English mathematician and philosopher said that *all* truths are tentative, partial, incomplete… and that thinking otherwise brings big trouble.

There are no whole truths; all truths are half-truths. It is trying to treat them as whole truths that plays the devil.

– Alfred North Whitehead

All this certainly demands humility, doesn't it?

Some religious minds see truth as eternal: time-tested, irrefutable, complete, and closed. An open mind is not so sure. Scripture, poetry, art, and literature ebb and flow over millennia in their power to console or satisfy. Yet anyone looking to scripture or art for *scientific* understanding may be several millennia out of date, and barking up the wrong tree.

An "enduring truth" is a good way to describe time-tested understandings of human nature, such as how to build community. Many religious teachings excel at this. Virtually every religion includes some form of the Golden Rule, to *treat others as you would like to be treated*. Yet even that might be updated for a more diverse, connected world. Others may not want to be treated as *you* do; why not treat them as *they* would like to be treated? John F. Kennedy used such wording in a 1963 Civil Rights address:

> *Every American ought to have the right to be treated as he would wish to be treated, as one would wish his children to be treated. But this is not the case.* — President John F. Kennedy

This formula raises another problem: I know a lot about how *I'd like* to be treated, but little about how *you* want to be treated. In following the best form of a Golden Rule, maybe first I should find out what you'd like.

Claims about enduring truth are deceptive if they insist that knowledge is settled, certain, everlasting, or absolute. We deceive ourselves if we believe such things. As one biblical scholar puts it:

> *If the truth is not open-ended, it is hypocritical to pretend to search for it.* — Robert Price

As a pre-Socratic Greek philosopher declared categorically (and ironically):

> *Nothing is constant but change.* — Heraclitus

What is Honesty?

Dictionaries define honesty as being *free of deceit*. But we've seen that humans deceive in so many ways, sometimes for good reason. It seems harsh to define as 'dishonest' all those deceivers – nearly all of us – whose behavior is so typically human.

Yet *respect* for truth persists even as we fail to live up to its demands. It's especially important to be aware of our own wishful thinking, blind spots, motives, weaknesses, and biases – and to be aware of them in others. With careful probing, we can shore up our own weaknesses, acknowledge where we've missed the mark, and repair what we've spoiled. We can be aware that we're likely to screw it up again tomorrow (and probably tonight as well). Repairing ourselves first seems far more reliable than what we can expect from trying to repair others.

Many words describe a person who *expresses* truth: honest, genuine, authentic, candid, credible, no nonsense, sincere… trustworthy.

Just as important are the qualities that help us *perceive* truth: wisdom, judgment, diligence, experience, skepticism, awareness… insight.

One of the 20th century's greatest moral leaders elevated truth and remarked on its essential role in freedom:

> *A friend once posed an intriguing hypothetical to Pope John Paul II. Suppose the entire Bible were destroyed. What one sentence or phrase would you want preserved for humanity's future? He didn't hesitate: "… the truth will make you free" (John 8:32). [This reflected his] conviction about the liberating power of seeing things as they are— and describing them honestly.* – George Weigel, author and scholar

A renowned Russian author responded similarly after the Tsar spared him from execution, at age 28, for literary offenses:

When I look back at the past and think how much time [I] lost in delusions, in errors, in idleness, in the inability to live; how I failed to value it, how many times I sinned against my heart and spirit — then my heart contracts in pain. Life is a gift, life is happiness, each moment could have been an eternity of happiness. Si jeunesse savait! [If youth knew!]
                                                      – Fyodor Dostoevsky

One of our biggest self-deceptions is in denying our own freedom and ability, today, tonight, and tomorrow, to choose differently and to improve. Our choices say much more about us than our assets, accomplishments, or abilities.

Each of us can choose more truthfully, more authentically, and simply better.

Honesty might be better understood not as freedom from deceit, but as:

> *respect for truth;*
> *courage in speaking truth; and*
> *fortitude in demanding truth.*

We all can admire that kind of honesty, especially when it's awkward or costly.

***

Reconciling honesty and deception

1. **Develop a 'personal radar' for your own motivated reasoning**. We can train ourselves to suppress our instinctive, defensive reactions to challenging or offensive statements. As with anger, counting to 5 or 10 can help our conscious mind catch up to our unconscious one. Notice the unspoken motivations and emotions surging beneath (and powerfully influencing) what we pretend to be happening, which is careful and rational thought.

2. **Try to have some patience with others who seem to have no idea how *their* motivated reasoning is doing a number on them**.

3. **When searching for details on something you believe to be true, add "debunked" or "false" to your search criteria, simply to see what contrarians are saying**. Not that the contrarians are right. Rather, a fresh choice is better than old thinking, assumptions, prejudices, and habits.

4. **Ask *disconfirming* questions, especially of someone spinning the truth.** (e.g., salesmen). This can curb a steady litany of what others think we want to hear, appealing to our own confirmation bias to support their goal. But be ready for incomplete, evasive answers! Example questions are:
   - What changed details would change your mind (or belief, or proposal)?
   - What other options haven't been considered?
   - What's the base success rate for those who've done what I'm considering?
   - What problems have occurred? What *could* go wrong? What *must* go right?
   - What circumstances could make this solution less effective or desirable?
   - Why do people return a product you're selling, or leave the job you offer?
   - What do critics or competitors say?
   - (More deviously) ask a question that embeds or assumes a wrong detail that's favorable to your spinner. Does (s)he correct a mistake from which (s)he would benefit?

5. **Restate disagreeable positions or beliefs in terms that opponents accept**. Ask them to do the same. This tactic alone diminishes straw men, hype, and other distortions. Achieve a first mutual agreement by accurately and fairly stating the conflicting positions. Others won't listen to us if we're unwilling to listen to them, or try honestly to understand. And almost nobody is persuaded when attacked, misrepresented, or misunderstood.

6. **Try to make friends of perceived adversaries (channel your inner Abraham Lincoln!)**. No one has ever been insulted into agreement.

7. **Identify and acknowledge unpleasant truths**. What are we hiding from, or afraid of? What do we know to be true, yet are unwilling to admit? What old, resilient problems could benefit from fresh approaches? Courage and forgiveness have great power to dissolve some of the embarrassment and pain we try so hard to avoid.

8. **Audit our own actions and beliefs for deception**. What things are so dear to us that we would distort the truth to preserve them? What are our deepest beliefs – and which of our beliefs may be delusions?

Further Reading

Jonathan Haidt	The Righteous Mind
Dan Ariely	The (Honest) Truth About Dishonesty
E.D. Hirsch	Cultural Literacy
Simon Blackburn	[various works on Truth]
Kim Scott	Radical Candor
Dallas Denery II	The Devil Wins: A History of Lying
Solzhenitsyn	Live Not By Lies

Now that we've probed three examples of deeply conflicted tradeoffs,
let's take a look at some tactics, strategies, ideas, etc. for resolving them.
A roundup is in Chapter 4.

Chapter 4 – Searching for Solutions

30 Actions, Techniques & Tactics for managing tradeoffs and conflicts

Simply **being present – face-to-face** – usually moderates how harshly we treat one another. We all have seen how rude people can be when they hide behind a media platform. So what kinds of actions and words best achieve a measure of reconciliation, connection, and mutually agreeable outcomes?

Chris Voss, a veteran hostage negotiator and teacher on negotiation, advocates **giving a small but symbolic bit of power to an opponent** early in a negotiation. Maybe let them unilaterally decide a term of engagement. A small show of respect or trust reduces the heel-digging and defensive walls that can be motivated by anger or fear. A tiny gesture of deference also shows that we're willing to **break old habits and tired routines**, and that we'll work to **avoid the misconceived dramas written by others**.

One other human right which is infrequently mentioned but which seems to be destined to become very important: this is the right, or the duty, of the individual to abstain from cooperating in activities which he considers wrong or pernicious. — Albert Einstein

To begin constructive encounters, we can **start the listening ourselves.** It's far more reliable than waiting for others. This means not just hearing while plotting a defense: it's listening **with undivided attention and engagement**.

Declaring a position creates resistance – "motivated reasoning" in action. 'Telling' shuts down the openness that could reveal points of agreement. But *asking questions* produces openings, possibilities, and connections. A great starting point is to ask what experiences have led to a belief that we may find strange. One of my young friends, in a college class on conflict management, was assigned a tense discussion AND required to *ask questions only*. He says the difference in tone was astounding.

By focusing on listening, reflecting, and observing, we don't talk so much. Think of it as a mysterious **voyage of discovery** – a chance to discover how a sensible person could believe something so at odds with our own outlook.

Even among friends, unrequested advice tends to be heard as criticism. Lecturing has a subtext: "I know better than you." But *asking* **for advice** signals respect and gathers information. According to a 2015 study, advice seekers are perceived as more capable, skilled, and qualified; the recipient feels valued for their knowledge and tends to return the compliment.

Test your own receptiveness to opposing views at https://receptiveness.net. This research-based assessment probes emotional balance, intellectual curiosity, respect for opponents, and tendencies to be offended or triggered.

One short phrase can change *know-it-all-ism* into a gentle, helpful nudge: "*Have you considered*" [*how your words would make Jane feel?*] [*what's needed to implement your view?*] [*what alternatives might be available?*].

In a less elevated mood, one of my favorite replies to a snarky critic is "*Oh, he speaks well of you.*"

Another simple phrase was used effectively by former Sen. Howard Baker, known for his moderation and gentility. "*You might be right*" powerfully disarms by appealing to an opponent's vanity. Defensive walls can tumble if we **acknowledge and explore competing priorities**. Deferential gestures signal that you're willing to listen and reciprocate rather than conquer. Hedge words ("maybe, tend to, might, could") take the sting out of differences. Other signaling phrases are *this is just my opinion, for what it's worth, this could be a bad idea,* and *maybe I'm wrong, but...* A well-phrased question (*Would it be wrong to say that...?*) gently hints at a tentative conclusion that's worth more discussion.

The opposites of such humility ("I might be wrong") are over-confidence, willfulness, and disregard for objections ("I'm completely and utterly right, get used to it"). It's worth **exploring how much confidence we have in what we believe**. "100%" is a poor answer: it refuses to admit any possibility of error. Answering 90+% suggests a need for critical reflection. Answers of 60-70% leave some room for discussion and exploration.

One tool for self-exploration is to ask: **what changes in facts or evidence would change my decision** about a "known" truth? Once again, a short or weak list shows a lack of reflection or critical depth, and a lower probability of respecting a conflicting view. Wherever we see righteous absolutism (in others, or especially within ourselves), we should invite Ms. Skepticism to the discussion table NOW – even if she's just a voice in our head.

Repeating (mirroring) what others say validates that we're understanding them correctly. If we sense that others aren't comprehending *our* message, we can ask them to repeat in their own words what they're hearing from us.

Diplomat Henry Kissinger, who literally negotiated war and peace, says American diplomacy sometimes features zeal to convert others rather than deeply listening to potential friends. **Americans tend to see negotiations in missionary terms**, trying to convert opponents rather than exploring their perspectives or needs. This bodes ill for stable outcomes, or "equilibrium:"

> *In my thinking, equilibrium [is] a kind of balance of power, with an acceptance of the legitimacy of sometimes opposing values. Because if you believe that the final outcome of your effort has to be the imposition of your values, then I think equilibrium is not possible.*
> – Henry Kissinger, former U.S. Secretary of State

Identifying and **checking motivated reasoning** is among the very most important takeaways from this book. We must recognize and manage it in ourselves, and (far harder) in others. Many people are completely unaware of their own subconscious, emotional, non-rational drivers of behavior.

A conversational gap can be filled with neutral statements like **Tell me more, I hear what you're saying, go on**… or with intentional silence that most people urgently seek to fill. Focusing on **discovery and learning** helps us to better **spot some agreement**, or simply to make an unusual friend.

Ridicule and scorn are tangible forms of disrespect that destroy community. They're weapons for battle. Senseless snark, often hurled for mere sport, says far more about the speaker than the person targeted. Potshots have a repellent subtext: *you aren't wanted here.* It costs little to be polite or respectful. Acting gracefully gives others a chance to show *their* best side; even if they decline, decency is an end in itself. One journalist's sharp observation about political friendliness extends to everyday social behavior:

> *Politics is a game of addition. Attract those who don't equate a*
> *glower with wisdom. What does good nature cost you? We should be*
> *able to conduct our lives without a constant air of menace. Our*
> *politics, also.* — Peggy Noonan

Being courteous to ill-mannered opponents is a smaller chore if we **understand the strengths of their case and the weaknesses of our own**.

Some offended or angry people believe that tactful behavior is inauthentic. Yet **decency and manners** lubricate civilized behavior. Authenticity doesn't require fierceness. Disagreement doesn't require being disagreeable. Though anger has a place, outrage usually looks like arrogance, and it often reflects poor self-control. An outburst may temporarily shut down an opponent, but it also destroys relationships. If we're the ones targeted by a rage, it can help to remember that the aggressor's subconscious motives could have little to do with us, or even with the dispute of the moment.

Expect positive outcomes. Even without agreement on the issue at hand, we can build relationships and lay a foundation for future improvements. Cognitive scientist Daniel Dennett describes the key steps, based on the work of Anatol Rappaport, for **composing a successful critical comment**:

> *You should attempt to re-express your target's position so clearly, vividly, and fairly that your target says, "Thanks, I wish I'd thought of putting it that way."*

> *You should list any points of agreement (especially if they are not matters of general or widespread agreement).*

> *You should mention anything you have learned from your target.*

> *Only then are you permitted to say so much as a word of rebuttal or criticism.*

A **default to respect** (or at least the appearance of it) quiets scornful attitudes. Respect gives a civil example and saves time lost to wariness. Few if any people feel respected by **negating words** like *shouldn't, can't, don't, not, no*. Similarly, **reasoning words** like *because, therefore, however,* or *although* can indicate a willful, unreceptive mind. Said more generally: arguing or lecturing hardens opposition; attentive listening softens it.

Justice may be defined by a fair process rather than a desired outcome. Using any means to get the outcome we want (or what we claim is "just") can itself be a serious miscarriage of justice, and a neglect of decency.

In his last commencement address as Harvard's President, Laurence Bacow emphasized listening habits: "*be slow to judge, and quick to understand.*" Less focus on what we plan to say helps us hear more of what others say. Active, receptive listening is an exploration. **Ask follow-up questions.**

If tempted by passion to lash out, a useful dividing line emerges by asking: *What good can come from this?* Is there any benefit other than vented emotions? Irate speeches or messages are better left unsaid or unsent. A ten-second delay lets our 'reasoning brain' restrain our 'lizard brain' from hasty, rash, destructive actions. The effort you would have spent on damage control can be applied to much more constructive purposes.

If we can't be fond, we can be kind. Nearly everyone wants to be heard, seen, known, welcomed, accepted, and respected. We can do this even amid hard disagreement. We can be kind to almost everyone. But if we think we can love everybody, then we just haven't met enough people.

Stop worrying about being liked. Be honest without harshness (as with the examples in the R-list below). Work instead to *deserve respect,* through self-discipline that reduces harsh or hostile behaviors. We can get along with people even if we don't like or agree with everything about them.

With more **curiosity**, even about things or people that seem wildly misguided, we can find more peace (or even friendship) amid the fray. We can find new ways to address problems while so much remains unsolved. We can work hard to **build community**, and even harder to preserve it. Maybe we should prioritize building solid connections and community, then over time use our newly produced goodwill to solve problems.

'Out of the box' tactics can soften standoffs. If friends and enemies are butting heads, converting some enemies into friends (or bringing outcasts into an inner circle) can reframe conflicts. Great Britain gave the Irish Republican Army a greater voice in Irish governance. General U.S. Grant adopted generous policies toward Confederates after the Civil War. Both sought to reconcile divided, alienated people into a greater whole. Even slight changes in "us" vs. "them" reframes boundaries. Simple yet creative tactics can break stalemates and dilemmas. Few of us will do this at a national or international scale. But each of us can do it with one person or a few people. Maybe then a small group, followed by larger ones.

Consider conducting a **tradeoff analysis**, which identifies and ranks the key parts of a tradeoff situation. After identifying the components, each member of a team (or discussion group) independently assigns a rating, say from 1 to 4 (or 5, or 10), for *how flexible* that component is to the team in reaching a solution. Where a business tradeoff analysis might look at cost vs. quality vs. timing vs. risk, a deep tradeoff analysis examines:

- **when or where** a value is more (or less) importantly followed.
- what **factors** might influence how stubbornly we insist on that value, or when and how we might compromise it.
- what might be **specific opportunities to accept** aspects of a competing value that erodes the value we favor?

If we feel stuck or cornered by aggressive remarks in conflicted discussions, it helps to have creative responses readily available. The "R-List" of categorized tactics (below) can help you do just that. Organized by University of California Professor Emerita Kathleen Kelly Reardon and published in *Harvard Business Review*, these tactics can help us avoid damage to important relationships and disarm threats to our credibility:

*Reframe — **Cast the issue in a different light.*** *Describe another person's words or actions in a way that behooves future interactions. If someone says, "I don't want to fight about this," a useful reframing is, "This is a debate, certainly not a fight. And you're a good debater, as I recall."*

*Rephrase — **Say the words in a different, less negative way.*** *If someone accuses you of coming on too strongly in a meeting, you might reply, "I was passionate." If you're described as stubborn, you could say, "I'm* very determined when something is important to a successful effort." Rather than let inaccurate or offensive words pass, suggest replacements.

<u>Revisit</u> — Use an earlier success to redefine a current failure. If the people involved in a conversation have a previous history of positive interactions, it can help to remind them of past success and their ability to find common ground: "We have a good track record working together. No reason to change that now."

<u>Restate</u> — Clarify or redirect negative wording. Anyone can inadvertently give offense or spark disagreement. At such times, it's useful to employ one of my favorite strategies: Give them a chance to do the right thing. "Surely there's another way to say that" or "Did you mean what I think I heard?" are useful ways to encourage a person to reconsider and alter what was said.

<u>Request</u> — Ask a question. If you doubt a person's intention, one sensible approach is to check your perceptions by querying [him or her] before reacting negatively: "Would you clarify what you meant just then?"

<u>Rebalance</u> — Adjust the other person's power. People cede power unnecessarily when they allow another individual to make them miserable or undermine their work. Often, such power imbalance can be changed. One way is to reduce the impact on you with your attitude — refusing to be upset — or by saying, "Fortunately, I'm not easily offended, especially by one-off situations like this."

<u>Reorganize</u> — Change the priority of the issues. Direct the conversation away from personal concerns by focusing on process. For example, one comeback might be, "We seem to agree on the what but are having some difficulty with the how." In this way, you cut the problem in half.

Often people choose *any* principle, strategy or tactic that can achieve a desired outcome. We might call this "pick your principle." Tub-thumpers rarely acknowledge a value or priority that conflicts with their own narrow favoritism and righteousness. They fail to see deep tradeoffs.

If in our frustration we're tempted to dismiss opponents as useful idiots – stooges who don't see the light – remember that contempt has a near-zero chance to improve anything. It's unproductive when (not if) our actions reflect these less-than-respectful thoughts. As we bemoan "them," they in their turn think were the tub-thumpers. Our first job is to make sure "they" are not correct, by doing a self-audit and checking it twice. Then we can work with decency and grace to **convert They into We.**

Let's remember that *enemies* are rarely converted by supposedly better ideas, even in defeat. *Friends* enlighten friends. We can persuade friends, as they persuade us, to see things a different and better way.

Think symmetrically. Look again at the discussion of symmetry in the Preface. Talk with friends about the benefits of mirrored thinking. *Deep Tradeoffs* arms us to **look for competing values that balance our own.** Balance makes us more able to find things we can respect.

We can relieve our anxiety over mere disagreement. We can **let go of urges to coerce** others into doing things our way. Instead we can focus our resistance on anyone who disrespects *any* person's freedom to live as he or she sees fit within an ordered system of liberty.

As we more skillfully balance values, maybe we can get Mary and John to go on a date. Or at least have coffee together. Some of the world's Marys and Johns are even married to each other. They've learned that **each human being is far more than a bag of enzymes with political opinions**. They know that such reductive thinking impoverishes our souls.

183

Conflicting Values in History

Binaries are age-old challenges; the perpetual clash of opposing forces is ancient, and historically persistent:

- Ancient *Greek tragedies* depicted the interplay of opposing passions or ideas. Dramatic conflict included a hero's struggle against a principle embodied in fate, a social norm, an inner demon, etc. Greek mythology also had oppositional conflict, as in sailing between Scylla and Charybdis -- a rocky shoal & whirlpool, a.k.a. 'a rock and a hard place.'

- The Roman god Janus represented a middle ground between polarities, such as past and future, barbarism and civilization, youth and maturity. Depicted with two faces, Janus was a god of beginnings and endings, gates and passages, transitions, time, and more.

- Asia's *Daoism* emphasizes an eternal interplay between yin and yang – dualistic forces in opposition, yet interconnected and interdependent.

- Jewish mystical thought (the *Kabbalah*) includes oppositional conflict, especially between finite and infinite.

- Persian religion, which is said to have influenced Jewish and Christian theology, emphasized the contest between good and evil. Popularizing historians Will and Ariel Durant said *"if history supports any theology this would be dualism like the Zoroastrian or Manichean: a good spirit and an evil spirit battling for control of the universe and men's souls."*

- A pre-Socratic philosopher, Anaximander, claimed some 2600 years ago that every material has an opposite (water has fire, earth has air). He said these opposites are continually at war. Socrates (about 150 years later) said truth lives within dialogue and dies when it's written down. In keeping with this, Plato left no writings and is known mostly by the works of his student Plato. The Socratic tradition of dialogue culminated in the 19th century "dialectics" of German philosopher Friedrich Hegel, who said historical progress is a repeating sequence of thesis, antithesis, and synthesis (or statement, conflicting statement, and resolution). Hegel's mistake was to conceive this process as leading to a grand historical resolution – which hasn't happened, and shows no signs of happening. Other philosophers like Kant, Mill, and Sartre are known for their work on moral conflicts and dilemmas. The premise you've read here in *Deep Tradeoffs* is that we can never reach final resolutions on a wide assortment of conflicting ideas and principles. In other words, there are no silver bullets – only perpetual (and hopefully skillful) management of conflicting ideas and impulses.

- Economists have long seen tradeoffs as a basic mechanism for managing competition and allocating scarce resources.

- Americans have been conflicted, divided and agitated from the country's earliest days: during its revolution to separate from Britain... before and during the Civil War, and the early 20th century Progressive movement... during the Civil Rights era... amid a pandemic... and during many booms and busts, cultural movements, and technological advances throughout history. We can take some comfort knowing that our country has survived much worse – though it always would be nice, in any season, to find calmer seas and better relationships.

- In the 20th century: psychologist Carl Jung studied the coincidence, tension, and union of opposites.

- 20th century socio-political theorist Isaiah Berlin proposed a theory of *value pluralism,* which says values can be both valid and incompatible. Such values can never be fully realized; they are a source of human tragedy and imperfection.

185

Is Finding Truth a Contest or Inquisition?

Among the American founders' legacies is our two-party system, which can be seen as another kind of check and balance. Though many founders were suspicious of two viciously dueling parties, the main alternative is a parliamentary system (as in Britain or Israel). There more points of view are organized into smaller factions. Then *after* an election, many minority parties must assemble a government representing a majority of votes cast. Parliamentary coalitions can be unstable. They fail unpredictably, forcing new elections. Democracy in pure form (i.e., direct political participation *without* representatives) may work at a small scale, but the large-scale alternatives to two or more parties leaves us with one dominating party, such as dictatorship, autocracy, monarchy, aristocracy, and communism. The math is simple: our choices are one, two, or many political parties.

America's two-party system, for all its faults, tends to force coalitions to form *before* an election, not after. A parliamentary system doesn't quell partisanship any more than two parties can do. Parliamentary advocacy just comes in more partisan flavors. Yet even these many flavors typically sort into two predominant orientations, toward active or limited government. If you doubt it, check out the British or Israeli media.

A similar legacy is found in the western legal system of two opposing lawyers (i.e. advocates), hammering away at each other in court. I once asked a professor why, in our Western legal system, lawyers paint such cartoonish caricatures of their opposition. His answer was brilliant: the main alternative is an inquisition. *One* point of view, usually in states governed by one dominating party that suppresses alternate views. Isn't that tyranny?

That professor's remark resonates with a tidbit from Aesop's ancient morality tales: *be careful what you wish for, because you might get it*. If you dislike the two-party system, you might dislike the alternatives even more.

Partisanship

If we wish for <u>no partisanship</u>, let's remember that quashing factions or prohibiting conflict requires a suffocating level of repression. It buries diverse opinions. Recognizing this once again reminds us that open societies have tensions in spades, between liberty and equality, unity and diversity, individuals and factions. Partisanship is one of the prices of liberty, as James Madison and other founders keenly recognized.

By the way: who would want a world where all agree to one way of being, or one view of life's meaning and purpose? Conformity and monotonous repetition would deaden us all; it would murder the spice of life.

For those of us who hate squabbling and bickering, let's be reminded that some outcomes are much worse than partisan disputes. Chief among them is an all-powerful government that tells citizens what priorities they must have, or what choices serve their personal interests. Such a government may be correct or incorrect – but its citizens are never free.

Restraint

In free societies, it's left to each of us to restrain behaviors in ourselves and in our friends. It's vital to refrain from behaviors that may be legal but are inadvisable. Examples include nasty confrontation, ridicule, offensive speech, or righteous arrogance that refuses to consider opposing views.

For those people we can't influence, walking away is usually a good option. Passing laws to restrain *disliked* behavior simply strangles our freedoms one notch at a time. Active conflict can be limited to resisting coercion, as any self-respecting person is likely to do. Our times call for less force and more persuasion – that is, persuading *and* being open to persuasion.

To paraphrase John Adams: we can't insure success, but we can deserve it.

***

Index of Quote Sources

315 quotes from 277 sources

Index of Topics

198

About the author

Mike Hassell is former General Manager and co-founder of audio publisher Knowledge Products. With degrees in engineering (Georgia Tech), business (Harvard), and liberal arts (Vanderbilt), Mike steadily pursues a broad range of interests, like the proverbial Renaissance Man. He's a veteran executive and board member of several dozen startups and early-stage businesses in information, health, biotech, and entertainment technologies. A native Tennessean, Mike's musical ability is quite modest compared to some of his neighbors. He has two adult children and lives with his wife in Nashville.

Conversations

Respectful, rich conversations are one of the best ways to build friendships. Consider picking a topic from *Deep Tradeoffs*, then plan a good talk.

The topic index is structured to expose key themes throughout the book. Most are great candidates for an enriching chat or extended dialogue. Another great guide is the thematic outline in the Table of Contents.

Please check in with us at deeptradeoffs.com.

We'd like to include you in future news!

You may have noticed on the cover that this is Volume 1.

Your comments and suggestions can help shape what's to come.

We'd love to hear your thoughts.

comments@deeptradeoffs.com

7|23

DATE DUE

JUN 28 2024			
			PRINTED IN U.S.A.

Made in United States
North Haven, CT
11 June 2023